Future Computer Opportunities

Visions of Computers Into the Year 2000

By Jack Dunning

Edited by Gretchen Lingham
Cover illustration by Lisa Mozzini
Art direction by Leah Steward-Shahan

First Edition Copyright © 1992
Computer Publishing Enterprises
P.O. Box 23478
San Diego, CA 92193
Toll Free (800) 544-5541

0-945776-24-1
10 9 8 7 6 5 4 3 2 1

This book is dedicated to
my wife, Pati, and our three children:
Richard, John-Mark and Cara,
who are the future.

Acknowledgements

There are a number of key people who aided me in the completion of this book, without whom the task would have been much more difficult and the ideas clearly more suspect. First my editor, Gretchen Lingham, who gathered information, software and hardware from manufacturers, while painstakingly working through my outlines and ramblings until something coherent emerged.

I would also like to acknowledge two individuals who took time out of their busy schedules to read a rough draft of this book from a technical standpoint, pointing out the areas that were complete rubbish: Roy Davis, and my brother, Joel Dunning. There are many other people who contributed to the ideas in this book, but Roy and Joel gave me the confidence that I was on the right track, because they both share a quality that I find extremely rare: vision.

Jack Dunning
Spring, 1992

Table of Contents

Foreword

Computers are built to ease the flow of information, but the flood of information about computers threatens to overwhelm all of us. Every day there are product announcements and magazine articles about a bigger hard disk drive, a faster microprocessor or a higher resolution monitor. Then there follows a slew of books on how to use these products in our work and at home. So why another book about new computer things?

Sometimes we need to step back and look at the big picture; climb the mast and catch a glimpse of the horizon through the fog. *Future Computer Opportunities* helps us to do this with the computer industry. This book doesn't claim to have all the answers: I don't think anyone has a road map of where modern technology will be taking us in the next few years, but in the past Jack Dunning has done a pretty good job of anticipating where the computer industry is going, and taking advantage of it.

Back in 1982 he and I were working at a military electronics company, realizing we were in dead-end jobs. Jack decided to do something about it, but it took him a while to figure out what. We had a few personal computers that we used for organizing parts lists, editing documents and general scientific work. The term "home computer" still referred to an electronic game that hooked up to your television set. Even the secretaries at work preferred their IBM Selectric typewriters over our computerized word processor.

Jack managed to pull together an up-to-date parts lists for our products by using a database manager program—taking less than two hours to sort the parts list. This was in a company that could never maintain a parts list at all. He then realized there was a future in bringing people and computers together to help them do their jobs better, and maybe even faster. Jack now brings computer information to people in a way that helps them use computers, even if they don't know the difference between a CPU and a RAM, and probably couldn't care less. Jack not only created a new career for himself with his computer magazine and book publishing businesses, but he created employment for more than two dozen other people—many of whom had no previous computer background.

So after 10 years of looking ahead, taking advantage of the way the computer has played a part in our lives, Jack has finally put down on paper his vision of where we are going next. I hope this book will stimulate you to think of future computer possibilities for yourself. You don't have to be a computer nerd to use the leverage of the computer's power to further your chosen career. Just as a hammer is a general purpose tool for the carpenter to pound nails, a computer can be your tool to handle your job in a more effective way—giving you the edge you need in this competitive world.

Roy Davis
February, 1992

Introduction

Looking back to 1980, I am truly amazed by the impact computers have made on our society. Since those early years of slow, expensive desktop machines, we have come to accept computers almost as readily as television sets.

My first computer was a then state-of-the-art box that cost about $2,600 by mail-order. Today you probably couldn't find a similar machine—but if you did, it would cost about $50. Back in 1980, it was unusual for someone to own a computer. Today, it's commonplace.

Some say that we've come about as far as we can. Sure, there will be smaller, faster computers, but the general consensus is that we will merely be doing the same old things faster.

This couldn't be further from the truth.

To date, the impact of the computer hasn't even scratched the surface of its potential. There are many new and exciting developments still occurring in computer technology, and the fruits of this technology will create more societal changes than most of us can comprehend. These changes brought about by computer technology will become the computer opportunities of the future.

There will be 10 to 100 times more entrepreneurial openings in the next decade than there were in the '80s—in all walks of life. For example, with the exception of very basic computer courses, our educational system is still virtually untouched by computers. Though the desktop computer has become increasingly popular, very few homes have been affected by one of the greatest benefits of the computer age: instant information. Even in the business world—where computers have been readily accepted—there are revolutions waiting to be sparked by triggers like pen-based computers.

Hundreds of opportunities are begging to be seized, and many of these prospects are staring us directly in the eye. Now, if we could only focus. . . .

Whose Opportunity?

You might expect computer programmers and digital engineers to be the ones foretelling the future of computers—after all, they know computers and have the skills to make the machines perform. But this kind of thinking is like expecting an oboe player to compose all the music and direct the arrangements for an orchestra. The oboe player may have talent, but the talents of composing and conducting are distinct from the talent for playing the oboe. The design of music is best left to those who have a flair for composition. The conducting of the symphony is the domain of those who have a knack for bringing the team together. The implementation of the details is the work of the "technicians," the musicians of the symphony. Generally, programmers and engineers will be the technicians, not the designers, of the future with computers.

Those who have the talent, background and experience to create a new future must be the ones to properly integrate computer technology as a tool for new solutions. In education, it may be the teacher who consistently graduates superior students. In health services, it may be a doctor or nurse with a gift for understanding the holistic health care picture. In law enforcement, it may be the police chief who can envision a new order for the future. These are the people who have the motivation and experience to properly define the problems, and visualize how computer technology will help solve them. Their vision will provide the path for programmers and analysts. Without the guidance of the occupational professionals, we may be building powerful computer tools that help solve the wrong problems. Or, worse yet, we may completely overlook using computers in new, innovative ways.

There is a place for everyone in this new future. Some people will be the designers who visualize the new uses for computers, coming from the most talented professionals within an occupation. Others will be the team builders who arrange and orchestrate the composition of technology. They may be from either the professional or the technical side of the new industry, yet they must understand both the technology and the industry. One such person could be a concerned parent who, following the guidance of a talented teacher, leads programmers and systems analysts in the implementation of a new classroom system. These managers bridge the gap between the occupation and the programmer. Additionally, there will be programmers and operators. The programmers implement the new design and the operators are the immediate beneficiaries of the new systems. The team is composed of varied talents from diverse disciplines.

Future computer opportunities are not limited to one group; rather, they cut across many lines, creating economic growth universally.

Types of Computer Opportunities

When people think about computer opportunities, they usually visualize the programming or selling of computers and computer software. There will certainly be vast opportunities in these areas, yet the potential room for new ventures goes far beyond those basic computer businesses. Many formerly non-computer-related activities will generate the new computer industries of the future. This is true for any of the emerging computer industries.

A new computer industry is triggered by the introduction of hardware that makes an application possible. Therefore, the first level of opportunity goes to the manufacturers and marketers of the hardware. The manufacturers have invested capital and resources over many years to develop the new hardware trigger, giving them a substantial lead over new entrepreneurs who plan to enter that part of the industry. By the time the new computer industry has emerged, only established manufacturers can be expected to have a reasonable chance to succeed.

The opportunities for the distribution and sales of the hardware can be more promising (especially if there are no established channels for the new hardware), but even these opportunities are small compared to what's available *within* the new industry.

With any new computer hardware trigger, there is mandatory software development. The hardware by itself rarely solves the computer problem. With the right timing, a small software company with a good product can grow rapidly into a large software company by producing software that supports an important new piece of hardware. Software development is an expensive proposition, but the demand for good software always outstrips the demand for the hardware it supports. Industry software is always a huge part of the new industry opportunities for software designers and programmers.

Software, though, is only a set of tools for completing a job. The job itself represents the largest group of opportunities in the new industry by far. Not only are consultants and trainers required to install the new industry, but the operators themselves are the direct beneficiaries of the new opportunities. The operators are the majority of the people who have new, more challenging occupations in the emerging technologies. The operators may be doctors, teachers, salespeople, politicians, criminal investigators, students or people from any other walk of life. The openings discussed in this book are for everyone—whether developers or beneficiaries of technology.

Identifying Opportunities

The seeds of the future are with us today. The technological instruments that will be the tools of the next 10 years are available right now—and at a reasonable price. Though many more new developments in computers will occur before the year 2000, their impact will not be felt until the next century. We are not waiting for new developments. All the pieces of the puzzle are on the table. The only thing needed is for astute players to properly match these pieces to create technological answers to societal problems. There are many players who are already puzzling together new technology to solve the old problems, but there remain many more problems which have been left unattended. These are the opportunities. But first, we must find new ways to look at our situations.

In the book *Future Perfect*, Stanley M. Davis points out that there are numerous solutions to old problems, but we tend to use the same old methods over and over again. The new computer opportunities require that we break out of our old ways of thinking and start walking the line of the non-traditional and improbable. Even the ways we use computers today must be questioned. Over our last 10 years of computing we have developed habits that hinder our growth toward the future. Many of our techniques and systems are obsolete, trapping us—we just don't know it, yet.

For example, we're taught that computers are tools for speed and repetition, relieving us of mundane, boring work. This is how we habitually approach applying computers to almost all our problems. But the computer is also a powerful tool for collaboration, creativity and interaction, capable of stimulating the human mind to great heights. By breaking the mind-set of how we *think* a computer should be used, we instantly create new opportunities. For example, a doctor could consult a laser disk–based diagnostic system to aid in the treatment of a rare disease. New information provides the physician with a new opportunity to develop a special treatment.

The purpose of this book is to provide a system for taking a new look at the possible future of computing. This book does not provide the answers, though there are many sample possibilities; it offers the questions. Your background and experience will yield the answers. You may find that the answers you supply are so stimulating and powerful that you want to drop everything and immediately change your career direction. On several occasions, in the course of writing this book, I was forced to grab myself by the neck and sit myself down, stopping myself from buying yet another computer system and heading off in another exciting direction.

This book only scratches the surface of computer opportunities, though it covers hundreds of suggestions. I'm only one person with limited experience. The real computer future depends on millions of thinking people with virtually unlimited combined experience.

You Design the Future

The first step to solving any problem is envisioning the end result. Once the goal is conceived, what remains are merely the details of implementation. The more people who see that vision, the easier it is to achieve.

As you read this book, see yourself as the designer of the future. Concentrate on your life pursuits, whether education, health, business or any other endeavor. Picture yourself 10 years from today. What are you doing? How are you using computer technology? What should happen with computers to create this vision? Which way would you direct the design of a computer system in your occupation? Don't worry if you find these questions difficult to answer. This book offers a system for creativity and stimulation. While reading, you will find insights into new and enlightening ways to use the new technology. These insights are what will make the system work for you. Without your brain power, the system will be empty.

To create your vision of a new future with computers you must understand:

- The computer and how it's impacting society today.

- The area of society you personally want to impact.

- Alternative ways of viewing the use of computer technology (i.e. collaboration, interaction, creativity, etc.).

- The computer hardware, which has the potential for triggering new industries.

- A system for cross-indexing your goals with the key computer concepts and the triggering technology.

Chapter One of this book is an overview of the computer's present impact on our society. Some of the changes induced by the computer are obvious; many less apparent. The changes are the result of technological and human idiosyncrasies meeting and combining, thereby adapting the strengths of both. Many of the influences of the computer are only just emerging, but the overriding trend is a shift from large power structures to networks of small specialized power groups, creating a more synergetic whole. In order to forecast, we must understand these effects and changes.

Chapter Two is an overview of the computer hardware that will be triggering the changes and new industries into the next century. Some of these triggers include older technology that is only now finding its mass market, and new technology that, when combined with other hardware triggers, creates still other industries.

Chapter Three is a look at our human endeavors and how they relate to computer technology. On a daily basis we strive toward our occupational goals. It is the nature of the human species to strive toward goals. We are driven to achieve. Without this drive we would shrivel up and die. The first step in moving toward a new future is discovering what motivates us most. A scientist may be obsessed by the potential of a new experiment. A teacher may be looking for new ways to capture the imagination of a student. The police may dream of new ways to protect citizens from crime. The person who achieves the greatest results is always driven from within. This chapter will help you relate computer technology to the achievement of your personal goals.

Chapter Four provides new and different ways of looking at what we do with computers now. In the context of *Future Perfect*, we are looking for new ways to view old problems. Offered is a different way of looking at computers and our daily endeavors, forcing us to view solutions in a new and innovative light. The concepts presented in this chapter represent non-traditional ways that computer technology can be applied to our occupations and productivity.

For example, in the next century, the classroom may have a network of computers, each communicating with the other. Each student would be working on a different part of a problem. As a proposed solution is developed by one student, it would be instantly shared with the other students via the networks. The other students could then collaborate on the possibilities and drawbacks of the proposed solution, generating and modifying still more solutions in the process. The machines handle the laborious communications while the students work their minds. *Collaboration, interaction* and *creativity* are the key concepts that make it possible to immerse the students in their own education.

Historically, new industries have been launched by the development of a specific new tool. These hardware tools are the key to triggering both new industries and societal changes. The computer is the most powerful mind-tool we have constructed. As more hardware tools are added to the computer, each of these pieces of equipment has the potential to trigger yet another industry. Each triggered industry changes society. Chapter Five of this book is about hardware triggers—how they work and how they fit in with our key concepts. Understanding the potential hardware triggers of the next decade is critical to predicting their imminent impact.

Chapter Six provides a quick, simple system for stimulating your vision of the future. It cross-indexes your chosen goals with the technology application concepts and the hardware triggers. The product is an explosion of ideas and directions emanating from your under-standing of the three.

The uniqueness of this book is that you will tailor its thoughts as you read it. The words and concepts of this book will suggest something different and distinct to each reader. This is a thought book. As you're reading and find your mind wandering, go with your chain of thought. The ideas your mind creates are far more important than the examples in this book.

In those thoughts are the seeds of the future.

Prologue

C hris sits staring out the window of his office, contemplating his next step. He's pondered his future many times over the last three years, but this time it's different. He's now made his decision and everything has been put into motion. Chris tries to recall when he actually decided it was time to act. It may have been three years ago when he realized there was no more room at the top of the company. It may have been last week when he turned in his resignation. No, there was no one clear decision point. Over the last three years Chris had created an irresistible force which had compelled him to move on. To resist that wave of events would have crushed him. There was no choice.

Three years ago, Chris was 38 years old and considered one of the outstanding prospects in the company. He had the ability to make things happen and, as a project manager, had built his reputation by turning around troubled programs. At every turn he was greeted with success. His coworkers considered it a pleasure to work with him. He always backed the people who did a good job for him. Chris had set his sights on the division manager's position, and felt that by age 45 he would have it well in hand.

At the time, he was being considered for the next step up between his present position and that of the division manager. But his bubble was burst when the company brought in someone from the outside to fill that position. Top management said they wanted some new blood in the company.

After 15 years of putting in 12-hour days and seven-day weeks, Chris now realized that he was in a dead-end job. It was as if Chris' entire future had been ripped out from under him. He enjoyed his work, but couldn't see himself doing the same job for the next 25 years. He knew in his heart that he had to find a way to leave the company. But he couldn't just quit—he had a family to worry about.

Chris was making excellent money, which only served to make matters worse. A move to another company would probably require him to take a cut in pay. Besides, who wanted to start all over again in another company, just to have the rug pulled out from under you?

Dreams of starting his own business were returning. Chris needed more control over his future; he was tired of his life hanging on other people's whims.

Over the next few years, Chris returned to school, learning more about the aspects of business in which he felt weak. He saved as much money as he could for the time when he would be on his own. He knew that he had to make his move within the next five years—if he waited longer, there wouldn't be enough time to make a business successful before the kids would need money for college. If he didn't jump before he was 43, he would be trapped for the rest of his life.

Chris was scared. He was afraid that he wouldn't have the guts to step out on his own. He was frightened of leaving the company's secure income. He agonized over his ability to make a business venture successful. But most of all, he was terrified of spending the rest of his life in a dead-end job.

To overcome his fears, Chris slowly cleared away his stumbling blocks. Going back to school erased one of his excuses for not starting a business. Buying a computer and working on it in the evenings mollified another excuse. Chris built walls at work which prevented him from turning back on his new-found course. He freely spoke his mind at all staff meetings, occasionally incurring the wrath of company management. He did the best job he knew how, but no longer compromised politically. Chris stopped working 12-hour days and seven-day weeks. His evenings and weekends were for his studies and his computer. Chris so carefully set his course that when the time came to leave the company, there was no longer any real decision to make. He had no other choice, and he was ready.

                                    *   *   *

Chris' story is not unique. It has happened many times over with only slight variations in the details. The theme is always the same. From age 35 to 45, men and women are faced with pivotal decisions about the direction of the rest of their lives. Prior to this age, they are too busy living life to worry much about it. Then, something happens to throw everything off course: an expected promotion is missed, a close friend of the same age dies of a heart attack, the time has passed to marry and have children.

No, there's nothing new about this story. The same thing has happened to every generation that has lived to reach middle age. What's different about today are the vast numbers of people who have reached this point in life.

If there weren't enough positions at the top for the generations of the past, the shortage will be even more severe for the Baby Boomers born from 1946 to 1964. In the 1990s, the youngest boomers will increase in age from 26 to 36. The oldest will age from 44 to 54, with the 35- to 45-year-old group growing the fastest. What appear to be dismal statistics for this generation's career opportunities are actually a blessing in disguise. These people and computer technology are the seeds for the most incredible entrepreneurial explosion in the history of mankind, beginning in this decade and not slowing until after the year 2010.

As the boomers reach the upper levels of today's companies, literally millions of talented and highly qualified people will be squeezed into the marketplace. These are not people who will merely stand in an unemployment line and fill out applications at another stodgy company. They are people who will want to take control of their lives and their future. These are people who will have the education, experience and talent to take charge.

In ordinary times, this could be a tragedy because there wouldn't be enough challenges for this incredible number of people—but these are not ordinary times. Technology and talent are crossing in a manner that bodes very well for the future.

This book is about technological opportunity in the next 10 years. As has been pointed out, there has been no lack of opportunity, only a lack of talent to take advantage of the opportunities. The talent to develop technology and business in the next 10 years will not come from the schools as much as from the corporations. The disenchanted members of the baby boom generation have already started—and will continue—to apply their abilities to the new technology, creating the vehicles that will change the face of society forever. As the next decade progresses, increasing numbers of this generation will move into the thousands of new computer niches, creating even more opportunities.

In the year 2010, regrets will lie with the people who stayed in the monolithic corporations of the '90s. They will say, "If only I'd known there would be so much opportunity . . . if only I'd taken the time to learn what the technology could do . . . if only I'd had the guts to do what so many others were forced to do by the times."

Not everyone who attempts to seize opportunity in the '90s will be successful. To be sure, there will be many mistakes and failures. But there is no doubt that there will be at least 10 times the number of successful business start-ups in the '90s as there were in the '80s. The technology and available pool of talent dictates as much. The only decision is choosing which will be worse in the year 2010: being able to say "I wish I hadn't tried that," or "If only I had. . . ."

Chapter One
Computers Changing Our Society

Knowledge Is Power

In early 1991, a Los Angeles resident with a home video camera taped a group of police officers beating a suspect, a man by the name of Rodney King. That videotape was broadcast worldwide as an example of police brutality in the United States. As a result, a number of the videotaped police officers were prosecuted for the act. Today police officers are a little more careful in their treatment of suspects. They never know when someone may be videotaping them.

Technology has placed another control on a traditional power structure. One person with a video camera can carry more power than a dozen police officers in witnessing the same event. It is the opposite of the Orwellian "Big Brother." "Little Brothers" everywhere are watching "Big Brother." The Rodney King incident is a vivid example of the shifting power base caused by new technology.

Throughout history, having knowledge that others don't posess has always been an advantage. On Wall Street, people called "insiders" are prosecuted for using knowledge to which only they are privy. Fear of the unknown, the greatest fear of all, is induced by a lack of knowledge.

People can gain more power by acquiring knowledge or be enslaved through their lack of it. It could easily be said that knowledge is the root of all evil—as well as the root of all good. Actually, knowledge is neither evil nor good. Those two moral attributes lie with the people who use the knowledge. As the saying goes, "Knowledge is power."

The computer is a tool of knowledge. It can collect, store and disseminate information. When tapped by people, the computer can supply information for human conversion into knowledge. The power of the computer is in offering up information. But only humans can convert that information into knowledge and, therefore, power.

Historically, our institutions have been built upon centralized power. Huge governments, huge educational institutions, huge corporations all wielding power through the careful control of knowledge. Even the media has become a huge, though uncontrolled, institution of rumor and suggestion, deriving power through the use (or misuse) of knowledge.

The behemoth computer of old came to symbolize the power of the institution. Sitting in its own air-conditioned room, cranking and twirling, it was the center of all institutional information. Only the blessed were given access to the sacred information, carefully converting the information first to knowledge, then to power. This was a safe, secure world until it started to crumble with the entry of the desktop computer.

The desktop computer has forever changed the structure of our society. If the computer is a tool of knowledge, therefore power, the desktop computer is a tool of *individual* power. When the stand-alone computer was able to move into the home, control of information changed hands and a series of transformations began.

In a central power structure, control is exercised by channeling all information through one central point. The data can be carefully screened and redistributed. Each computer represents an information point. The more information points, the more difficult it is to control information.

The desktop computer has created so many information points that it is literally impossible to control information. The central power structure, which depends on knowledge control, has become an archaic relic of the past. Many of these central power structures just don't know it yet. They include centralized businesses, educational institutions, medical organizations and governments. The next decade and beyond will see the continued disintegration of large, centrally-controlled power structures of any type.

The implications are enormous. If these structures that have operated society for the past centuries become obsolete, what new forms will succeed them? There are a few concepts that may shed some light on future power structures and help to discern the impact of the microcomputer.

Ready Information

Computers are putting information at our fingertips. We can get baseball scores without listening to the radio for a half hour and wading through those inane commercial messages. The value of the commercial time drops as the listener response drops. A small piece is taken out of the power structure of the major radio networks.

We can stay at home and use our computer to shop for college classes around the world, tailoring our curriculum to our needs. The educational system fragments a little more.

Before going to the polls, we can use our computer and a modem to check the voting record of all the candidates. The massive media campaigns are diluted by a slight degree.

From many people's point of view, there could be too much information available—too much dirty laundry hanging on the line. Yet technology has made this trend inevitable. Information will run amuck. David will compete with Goliath. Society will fragment and specialize.

Fragmenting Institutions

Small businesses now compete with the industrial giants through decentralized knowledge. Today, the largest share of the computer market goes to a group of computers called IBM clones. Individual retailers buy computer parts and manufacture their own computers in back rooms. They own no factory, but present severe competition for the big guys. Despite predictions that these small, independent dealers would never survive, they are growing at a healthy rate while the major chains are suffering. What is their advantage? Knowledge.

Our institutions are splintering and fracturing into smaller units of power. Each unit has relatively little power, but the combined power is greater than that of the major institutions.

As an example: Not long ago, the National Football League threatened to scramble game broadcast signals, forcing pubs and sports bars to pay fees to show games to their customers. The pub and bar owners threatened to drop Budweiser beer, a major NFL television and radio sponsor, from their fare. The signals were never scrambled. This was the power of knowledge.

The computer has made it too easy to use knowledge. With a

computer and a laser printer, a graphic artist can open a low-overhead advertising agency to compete with the major, high-priced agencies. An engineer can do free-lance designing and earn much more than by working for one company full-time. A writer can publish his or her own book without depending on the good graces of a major publisher. It is foreseeable that small businesses will one day design and build their own line of competitively priced automobiles marketed against today's major automobile manufacturers—all through the clever use of computers.

Educational systems are beginning to break up into smaller-sized units, tailoring education to the student while providing a stimulating interactive environment. The students are no longer required to live on campus or attend classes at a set hour, yet they get the full value of the classroom experience. Small is a key word in the future of organizations. There is no synergy in enormous structures created by merging huge corporations. The synergy comes from the smaller, specialized units interacting with other small, specialized units—each doing what it does best.

Large institutions will disintegrate through their own expertise. The computer relieves the expert of dependency on the large institutions for a livelihood. Today's tools make it possible for the individual to sell his or her knowledge on the free market. In record numbers, experts are leaving the nest to start their own small businesses, leaving the large companies to rent out their individual expertise, often to the same company, at a higher price. The computer is behind all this. As small business becomes more competitive, big business becomes less competitive.

Changing Working Relationships

As the huge power structures begin to crumble, society will develop news ways to get work done. The individual will no longer be able to depend on the large institutions for security and protection. It was once believed that the United State's coal, steel and automobile industries were institutions that would outlive eternity. If someone had a job in one of those occupations, they were considered set for life. Today, we find no security in large-sized institutions as huge numbers of lifetime employees join the ranks of the unemployed. In fact, the large institutions' inability to regroup and reorganize has doomed its future and that of its workers.

The future requires smaller, more adaptable organizations that can change direction quickly and effectively. More small units are taking over societal functions. Rather than colossal organizations built to complete colossal tasks, small groups of experts are being utilized in modular units, applying their power to particular problems. These units require an unprecedented level of communication with other working units in their efforts to solve the most complicated problems. There is a growing need for collaboration and sharing of information. As systems grow, this need for a fluid network of working relationships grows. This is changing the nature of all our interpersonal relationships.

The concept of "working relationships" becomes more important than "senior-subordinate" relationships. Information moving sideways, from peer to peer, becomes more significant than information moving vertically. The power is transferred to the gathering points. As the goal of completing the task becomes paramount, the project managers, rather than the functional department heads, become the central focal points.

The necessity for interpersonal skills grows as people find that they must manage without having the "formal" power to do so. Work being done through networks requires constant attention to relationships. Society is moving away from a structure orientation to a relationship orientation.

Because complexity and ambiguity become more prominent, working groups must specialize even more. Specialization forces us to develop stronger working relationships with other specialties. Collaboration rather than command will be the primary mode of operation.

Visualize a web of small units of business or work. They merge temporarily to work on specific projects, then break apart and recombine to create new task forces. Each is autonomous, making its own project decisions, yet collaborating with the other units as required by the work. The relationships between the units dominates decisions. Those units that both perform well and handle "working relationships" well are the most successful.

Family Roles and Technology

The computer is the tool of both greater family isolation and greater family collaboration. If left to its present position of isolator and captivator, the computer will continue to be a source of family withdrawal and separation within the home. Only when the computer is turned into a tool of collaboration will this trend be reversed, adding to family communication and life.

"Can't it wait until a commercial?" This is a statement of isolation. The television's emergence in the last few decades has created a detachment within the family. Family dinners have become an event of the past, and children learn their morals from Saturday morning cartoons. Sadly, rather than offering an immediate solution to this problem, it appears that computer technology has initially made the problem worse. Video games and other one-on-computer-type exercises have been even more intrusive on family life than television, creating greater isolation. This will not change until the computer becomes a tool of family collaboration. The entire family could be using the technology to work toward common goals. The computer network could become a source of greater family interaction. Though the tools are there, this has not happened—yet. Collaborative games or educational tools could and may be developed that require the interaction and teamwork of family members via computers and local area networks. Without some level of innovation, the family structure will be doomed to the same disintegration as other structures of society. What will there be to take its place?

Computers and the Consumer

If you own a computer and a modem, you can get up-to-the-minute shopping information. For example, Prodigy, an on-line service that can be accessed from most desktop computers, gives buying information on a range of goods and services, from airline travel to computer products. With on-line shopping, it's easier for a customer to do comparison shopping without leaving home. In the next decade, video, audio and text will be combined to produce on-line catalogs to be used at home. A customer will know a good price before ever entering a store to shop.

Information is power, and the computer will bring that power to the consumer. Businesses will be forced to work smarter because computers will make the competition stiffer. It will be much easier for a buyer to find the right product at the right price. Price competition will be stiffer. There will be more discount businesses, and service will be a commodity purchased separately. Just as the automobile industry has separated sales and service, most businesses will be forced to do the same. This will be a problem for many businesses, but an opportunity for many others. On-line buying services will become available for all products and services. Businesses will advertise with these services, just as they advertise with magazines today.

Smaller businesses will be price-competitive with large businesses through flexible, inexpensive marketing schemes. Many of the advantages of mass-producing a standard product will disappear. The computer allows economies of scale without massive production runs, even at quantities of one. Consumers get more of what they want —at the right price—from smaller, more flexible businesses.

The middlemen of the future will be computers coupled with rapid delivery services, taking orders directly from customers via computer and instantly forwarding those orders to the manufacturer. There will be no distributors required to carry inventory or maintain a huge staff. The middle layers of commerce will be absorbed at both ends. The price will be lower for the consumer and the profit margin higher for the manufacturer.

The Media and Technology

The way we receive information will change. The volume of world news is so large that it is virtually impossible for one person to hear or read the news that is most important to him or her. As huge and powerful as today's media is, it is sorely inadequate to the task before it. We get snippets of news that leave us in a state of emotional ignorance. Semi-experts are quoted creating uncontrolled public outrage over factoids that most members of the media cannot comprehend themselves. There are huge gaps in the news if editors do not deem information "newsworthy." The times are so complex that there is no convenient source of information that will give us the uncluttered facts. There isn't enough space in the newspaper; there isn't enough time on television. Often, "getting the scoop" on the story has become more important than reporting it accurately.

Fortunately, this will change in the coming decades. Computers will provide the detailed facts that we need without the editing of today's opinion makers. The breakdown of power structures will hit the media, as well. People will turn to more independent sources of news and information. In many cases it will be the actual words and thoughts of experts and witnesses and not the watered-down version delivered by reporters.

In the next century, people will get their news from the computer. (Such news services already exist and are used on a small scale.) This news may include sound and video clips, but most importantly, it will include current information. After sitting down at the computer, the user will be able to call a database that is dedicated to collecting and organizing news. The reader will select the topics and the depth of reporting required, in many cases being able to read the actual transcripts from eyewitness reports and experts. The user will get the depth of a newspaper with more timeliness than a local radio broadcast. Ultimately, both video and audio will be combined to provide the reader with a multimedia, interactive electronic newspaper.

Who Is Going to Do It?

These changes are already upon us, though many of them are only in their early stages. As this transition to a modular society proceeds, there will be numerous problems created. Each of these transitional problems creates an opportunity for another small unit of endeavor: a group of people who have the skill, foresight and talent to apply the new technologies to the solution. As working groups become smaller, they need better tools for communicating with other working groups. As crime threatens our homes, we need better devices and techniques for securing ourselves. As the economy of knowledge requires our children to learn more, we need new approaches and instruments for education.

There is no shortage of future computer opportunities. There is no shortage of money to take advantage of the opportunities. There is no shortage of technology to bring the opportunities to fruition.

Everything is in place to do the job, except the labor: the labor that understands how the computer works, the labor that understands a problem well enough to envision a solution, and the labor that is motivated to create a solution with computer tools. The demand for good programmers, system designers and hardware experts will far outstrip any possible supply in the next 10 years. There are 1,000 times more potential ventures for computer users than there are people to start them. And this is probably a gross underestimate: Demographics predict a general shortage of graduating students entering the labor market.

How do we get the job done if we don't have enough people? The answer must be that the labor will come from all walks of life. The teacher will become the system developer. The law enforcement officer will become the programmer. The social worker will design new ways to computer-assist clients. The application and labor must originate at the most productive level: on the line where experience gets the work done. The implication is that many members of the baby boom generation will begin new careers based on computer technology during their mid-life years. There is evidence that this is already occurring.

This trend began with the introduction of the desktop computer into the home. Typically, the machine is purchased by a working professional, 25 to 35 years of age. Evenings and weekends are spent experimenting, inventing and developing new ways to accomplish tasks. Eventually this work pays dividends, and in numerous cases a new business is spawned. This trend of entrepreneurship is underway, but it is only in its infancy. In the next decade there will be a tremendous upswing in this movement, and by the year 2000 most of the experts in applying computer technology will be laymen who started out of their homes years before.

This self-education trend is part of our unmeasured economy. It is a massive capital investment of time and equipment that is recorded by no economic statistics. It is an effort that moves forward at a continuous rate with no letup. It is not dependent on any business, government, educational institution or any other major power entity. It is dependent only on the inexpensive, readily available power of the computer.

The commonly asked question will be, "Where did that innovation originate?" And the most common answer will be, "In someone's garage."

The future is on the way. It is one of fragmenting power structures and smaller entities networked into a larger, yet more powerful and flexible web of effectiveness. It is a future in which the individual finds more control over his or her own destiny as technology shifts the power away from large institutions into the hands of individuals. It is brought to us by the people who have the ability to visualize the new reality.

In order to envision the new future, it is important to understand what can be done with the technology. What are the possibilities? The next chapter is an overview of the hardware that is available to create many of the new opportunities.

Chapter Two
Technology and Hardware Triggers

Information is the blood of our society, and the vitality of our systems is dependent on its flow. The technology of information is built around its flow and storage. Today's hardware has been used primarily for business applications, but the potential for industries in areas not traditionally considered is virtually unlimited. Today, there exists hardware which, when combined with the appropriate software, has unique capabilities for triggering these new industries beyond the next decade. The best part is that this hardware is designed, produced and available at a very reasonable price. This is not equipment that we must wait to see: It is here today.

Computers have been with us for decades, desktop computers for a little over a decade. Computers are accepted as tools for our future and as a key to our new industries. Yet we need a little more than a computer for the emergence of new opportunities. We need a technological or economic breakthrough that will act as a catalyst and ignite a new computer industry. This breakthrough comes normally in the form of a hardware trigger that makes a new tool out of an old computer. With the exception of pen-based computing and some multimedia discussions, a certain type of computer is not important. Most new applications can be performed on any computer platform with enough power and storage. The emphasis is on those hardware triggers that, when combined with a computer, are likely to trigger new opportunities in the next 10 years.

Computers and Operating Systems

There are two types of computers competing for dominance on the desktop in the next century. The first is the well-known Personal Computer (PC) which includes the Apple Macintosh and Commodore Amiga. These computers are inexpensive and well within the budget of most middle-class consumers. These are the most pervasive computers, tending to dominate the movements of the computer market due to their sizable numbers. As they become more powerful, they will encroach on the high-end computer market. Most PCs operate under MS-DOS, the operating system that denotes IBM-compatibility. The jury is still out on which operating system will dominate the PC market, though most feel that it will be a *Windows*-type environment in which multiple programs can be run simultaneously. But the choices in the next decade will not be limited to PC operating systems.

Less well-known to the general public are the computers commonly used in engineering firms for more sophisticated applications like Computer Aided Design (CAD): workstations. Historically much more expensive than PCs, workstations include many powerful features that make them ideal for the time-consuming, data-intensive uses in engineering and science. In the early part of the '90s, workstations have already shown dramatic drops in price. At this writing, a workstation is priced at a little more than twice the price of a similarly equipped 80486 PC (the top of the line in personal computers). Even so, the performance rating is about five times that of the PC, making the workstation a much better performance buy.

Most workstations operate under UNIX, the older, proven AT&T operating system. UNIX has become the standard for workstations, and there are huge software bases to support it. There are many advantages to UNIX: It's free, it's easy to enhance and add value to, it includes built-in communications (i.e. networking), and there are a great number of companies supporting it.

The world of more powerful personal computers and less expensive workstations seems to be on a collision course in the 1990s. If the workstation comes to dominance, which is highly possible, UNIX or some form of UNIX will probably become the dominant operating system. If the massive size of the PC market overwhelms the workstations with inexpensive, more powerful machines, who knows what the operating systems of the future will be! In any case, all computers are evolving toward a *Windows*-like environment, whether *DOS-Windows* for MS-DOS machines or *XWindows* for UNIX machines. The hardware technology core of future computers, however, is likely to come from the powerful workstations.

Decisions on technology selection must be made based on what will do the best job at the right price—the lowest cost for the best performance. Any other method of equipment and software selection is folly. Given that any hardware will run most software in the future, price and performance criteria will drive hardware-buying decisions.

Today, however, most software will *not* run on just any computer. You have to select your computer based on software availability for that machine. Otherwise, you're leaving too much to luck. That's only for gamblers. True entrepreneurs are not gamblers. They always play with a stacked deck.

The Macintosh is caught in the middle of all this chaos. The unique advantages of the Macintosh may soon be wiped out by PenPad-type computers, and the less-expensive—yet technically touted—Amiga computer. The Mac has been left crushed between less expensive workstations and omnipresent PCs. While the Mac presently has a lead in multimedia applications, Commodore's Amiga is the machine of choice for many professionals who create video animation. The power of the MS-DOS machine lies in its flexibility and adaptability. Though the multimedia capabilities of the PC are relatively meager at this writing, its expandability could rapidly change that situation. Apple's leadership has some very tough decisions to make in the next few years, and those decisions will determine its future in the next century. The rumor is that Apple is developing a new operating system that will run on every type of computer, large and small. Who knows? Apple may provide the operating system of the future!

Both Apple Macintosh and IBM-compatible computers are single-processor computers, meaning that almost all of the computing work is done via the sole main processor. The problems with the single-processor computer are becoming more evident in this decade. Even with the more powerful microprocessor chips, as long as one processor alone is doing the bulk of the work, there is little noticeable improvement over older chips. Future applications like multimedia demand multiprocessor computers. At least temporarily, this has given the Commodore Amiga a technological advantage in markets like desktop video. The Amiga has six to eight separate processors to handle different functions of the computer. This is why the Amiga offers such impressive animation displays when compared to both

Macintosh and MS-DOS computers. The computers of the year 2000 almost certainly will not look like the computers of today. Pen-based computer systems and multiple processors will have a tremendous impact on the look and performance of these new machines. The operating systems of the year 2000 may be a variation of today's systems or a completely new development.

For a designer of future computer opportunities, operating systems and computer types have only partial significance. When better technology comes on the market, the bridges are usually built-in. People are reluctant to give up their MS-DOS computers because of the vast amount of software available for those IBM-compatibles. But newer computers, like Amigas and the IBM OS/2 machines, work to maintain some level of compatibility. In the Amiga, an MS-DOS-compatible board can be added, and OS/2 machines can run both MS-DOS and OS/2.

When a new project is begun, it's important to select the best technology available for the task at the best price. In five years it may be best to switch to the latest computers and equipment, but to delay the launching of the new endeavor until better hardware is available would be foolish. Valuable time and experience would be lost, and both of those qualities are unrecoverable. Move ahead and let the technology catch up with you.

Hardware Triggers

In the computer world, new industries are triggered by a technological breakthrough, usually in the hardware. That evolved hardware supplies the missing link to solve a problem and creates a market for the solution. The new industry includes the production of the hardware trigger, the growth of the software businesses that support the industry, and the new application itself—the largest portion of the industry. If it's possible to identify the hardware triggers of the next decade and understand the problems to be solved, it will be possible to identify the emerging industries.

One example of a hardware trigger is the laser printer. Laser printers are computer printers that can produce high-quality output of both text and graphics. Prior to the mass introduction of the laser printer, computer graphics were printed on dot-matrix printers. Letter-quality printing was accomplished on separate typewriter-like printers called daisy wheels. The quality was poor on the dot-matrix printer, but the daisy wheel was unable to produce graphics.

Laser printers capable of producing both high-quality graphics and text have been available for many years, but they've always been horrendously expensive. In the mid 1980s, the price of laser printers began to drop dramatically. As a result, it was possible for users of desktop computers to take advantage of the laser printer features that combine high-quality text and graphics. New software companies sprung up that provided software to the desktop computer that would in turn control the output to the laser printer. A new industry called Desktop Publishing (DTP) was triggered by the introduction of these low-cost laser printers.

Types of Hardware Triggers

The focus of this book is the desktop computer and the hardware equipment that will bring about new computer industries. This is not to slight the applications involving mainframes and supercomputers —those uses will certainly be significant. What distinguishes the desktop computer is its low cost and mass availability. The opportunities in desktop computing are accessible to virtually everyone with any desire to take advantage of them. The hardware triggers are just as accessible, and the cost will rarely be a major roadblock. (The hardware triggers are grouped according to function and discussed in more detail in Chapter Five.)

Communications

The flow of information is called communications. In the 1980s, communications remained just a small part of computing, with the modem being the primary tool for communication between computers. Within the business environment of the 1980s, Local Area Networks (LANs) connecting PCs became increasing popular for intercomputer communications. Yet by the end of that decade, less than 10 percent of computers in business were attached to a network. Most desktop computers were stand-alone systems.

Modems

In the 1990s, computer communications will be one of the hottest growth areas. In 1991, the modem was already outselling the computer by a factor of three to one, creating a new market of modem users. In spite of the problems with modem communications, the modem will come into its own in this decade as a hardware trigger. In the next century, the modem will fall by the wayside as better, faster direct-connect fiber optic technology and digital cellular technology will eliminate the need for the modem.

Local Area Networks

Local Area Networks (LANs) are in their infancy as human collaborative systems. Most applications installed have been in the business world, but in the 1990s the synergy derived from a network of computers will be applied to many more occupations. Today, small LANs that connect up to three PCs are available at a very reasonable cost. The power and flexibility of the computer network will be felt in home applications, education, entertainment and many other non-business areas.

Voice Mail

Voice mail is a system for computer-based answering machines. As a human form of communication that can be easily accessed by the telephone, voice mail is already creating profitable businesses. There are systems that are using voice mail as a dating service. Many businesses have replaced the receptionist with voice mail. Bank inquiries are routinely answered by voice mail. Many other systems disseminating information via voice mail will start up in the '90s. Restaurant, sports, entertainment, retail buying and shopping information are just a few of the opportunities that are available.

Fax

The fax machine has already stood the business world on its head. In many businesses it has become the primary means of communication. Boards are available for most computers that will allow the computer to act as a fax. The application of fax machines in the next 10 years will continue to grow.

Fiber Optics

Fiber optics have almost replaced satellite and microwave communication for long-distance services. For the desktop computer, fiber optics will be a major technology trigger for the next century. Though it is not expected to have major commercial impact on the desktop computer until the year 2000 (it will take at least that long just to cable cities with fiber optics), fiber optics will no doubt make possible many of the communication dreams of the future—including eliminating the modem for most applications.

Information Storage

The key to many occupations is the immediate availability of information. That ready access to information requires storage. Data storage technology has made tremendous strides in the last decade, increasing the capacity and speed of hard disk drives.

The Hard Disk Drive

The hard disk drive is the backbone of desktop computer storage. This decade is providing us faster drives with capacities in the gigabyte (1,000,000,000 bytes) range. Since the hard drive is integral to all computer systems of the future, it will not be discussed as a separate hardware trigger. It is required for almost all the opportunities presented in this book.

The Laser Disk Optical Drive

In the next decade, laser disk technology will come into its own. Now with rewrite technology, the greater storage capacity of the laser disk with removable media will trigger vast new industries, especially in the areas of entertainment, education and research. The laser disk technology of the CD-ROM has already seeded the early stages of a new computer technology.

Mobility

In the late '80s and early '90s, the laptop computer was generally considered the machine for the mobile executive. The laptop computer is a scaled-down version of a desktop computer. Eventually the laptop brought about offspring called palmtop computers. Usually weighing less than a pound, the palmtop computer was scaled down to a size slightly larger than a checkbook. Palmtops have been used in many mobile professions like insurance sales, but their small keyboards and screens have made them impractical for most applications. Laptop and palmtop computers have acted as a stopgap solution to the computer mobility problem, which will ultimately be addressed by PenPad-type computers and remote communications.

PenPad-Type Computers
Though not a desktop computer, the PenPad-type computer—working in conjunction with the desktop computer—will take the '90s by storm. Possibly one of the most exciting developments since the introduction of the desktop computer, the applications and opportunities of PenPad systems are almost endless. PenPad will bring an entirely new meaning to the term "portable computer," showing the world a truly easier way to compute: as if using a pen and clipboard. These systems will expand computers beyond their niche as almost exclusively a white collar tool into the world of the blue collar worker.

Cellular Systems
Wireless networks and cellular communications will further increase the mobility of computers. High-quality wireless computer communication is already on the way. Digital cellular technology is already developed to expand capacity over analog mobile telephones. Transmission of computer data via digital cellular systems will be faster and more error-free than even today's wire-line modems.

Visual Information
The '80s have given us higher-quality digital displays, though outside the graphic arts field, the value of their uses to date have been meager. In the 1990s, the integration of laser/video technology in multimedia will bring high-quality systems to the market in entertainment, education and training. Laser printers will continue to drop in price, eventually becoming everybody's printer of choice.

Video Toaster
One likely visual hardware trigger is NewTek's Video Toaster,

built for the Amiga computer. This piece of equipment turns a low-cost Amiga computer into a home video editing system, complete with 128 different video effects. The Video Toaster may do for Amiga and Desktop Video (DTV) what the laser printer did for desktop publishing.

Audio Information

Audio uses for the computer were almost non-existent until the late '80s. Now music and sound effects are common for adventure games, and have become an integral part of educational and entertainment software.

Sound and Music Cards

Sound and music cards will become standard equipment on computers, especially for entertainment and education. The computer could become the core for home entertainment in the next century. Certainly the applications that offer voice, text, graphics and music will be in demand in the '90s. Everything from reading and language tutoring to high-quality music will benefit from sound and music capabilities.

Voice Mail

A computer that answers the telephone and dispenses information is called voice mail. It is here today and offers tremendous opportunities to those who wish to pursue them.

Voice Recognition

Voice recognition has tremendous potential as an input device for a computer. A person can speak faster than type. But the technological problems of voice recognition will limit its use to highly specialized areas. Many audio applications come more from a fascination with technology than a well-thought-out solution. One post office planned to use voice recognition technology to eliminate the need for one person to call out zip codes on mailbags while another person keyed in the code. With voice recognition only one person would be required to call out the codes and the computer could capture them. Though this would be a clever use of voice recognition, it would be much simpler for the Postal Service to go to the more accurate and commercially popular barcode and scanning system.

Multimedia

Multimedia is one of the new computer industries of the '90s that is composed of a number of hardware triggers. The dominant hardware trigger is the CD-ROM (Compact Disc–Read-Only Memory), based on laser disk technology. The CD-ROM provides the storage capacity required to combine digitized video and audio on one removable optical diskette. This will be the platform for interactive entertainment and education. The complete system will also require a sound card, high-quality color graphics, a hard drive and a semi-powerful computer. This will be the system to own in the next decade, creating enormous opportunities for multimedia applications.

These hardware triggers are available today, and most important, they are reasonably priced. Some of our triggers, like the modem, have been around for decades, but have been missing the proper consumer market. Others, including local area networks, are widely recognized for their value in business, but have had little introduction to non-business areas due to a lack of understanding of their potential. Hardware triggers like PenPad-type computers are here, but won't have their major triggering effect until the mid-'90s due to the time it takes to introduce applications software.

For the purposes of most people reading this book, the operating systems and computers used in the next decade will be of little consequence—they're all headed in the same direction. The hardware triggers will be available on all systems, and the fundamental opportunities will not change. If you start out on a system that later falls into disfavor in the marketplace, the switch shouldn't be too difficult—though it might be costly if your application designs are too heavily dependent upon a dying system. There are ways to protect against this by selecting hardware and software that is easily transportable to other systems.

The hardware triggers emphasized in this book are by no means the only technologies that will have dramatic impact on our society and the way we do business, but most of the other breakthroughs will not take off into new industries until after the year 2000.

Hardware triggers work in combination with the computer, and often other hardware devices. Many of the new industries created will be dependent on the proper combination of hardware, often including multiple triggers, as is the case with multimedia. In our exploration of possibilities we will not limit ourselves by merely considering one device at a time, but we'll have to limit ourselves in the number of possible combinations we consider. Also, you must draw upon your own experience and consider your own occupation in the context of my examples. It's up to you to identify the problems that can potentially be solved by computer technology.

This chapter has been a brief introduction into hardware triggers. The next chapter is a look at some of the places where we can apply our hardware triggers.

Chapter Three
The Future of
Computers in Our Life Endeavors

In the 1980s, the desktop computer took the business world by storm. Businesses developed the first PC applications and created a market that continues to dominate the computer industry. In the last decade, small start-ups turned into mega-corporations, dominating the software industry. Names like MicroSoft, little known before 1980, are giants by anyone's standards today. Computer opportunities in business are crowded with well-financed behemoths. In the 1990s, computer opportunities will diversify outside of traditional business uses. The computer will explode as an entertainment device. Health and medical uses for computers will become increasingly important. Applying computers to the crime problem and environmental issues will help resolve much of the political debate. Education will be a major growth industry for computers, aiding in the lagging productivity of today's school systems. And, of course, the growth of business applications is not at an end. Professions and occupations that previously had difficulty integrating the power of the computer into their work will find that the new technology will provide amazing progress in productivity.

The purpose of this chapter is to take a look at some occupations that have great potential for computer applications. Possible future scenarios begin each section, but don't limit yourself to the occupations or examples presented here. There are many more possibilities that you're probably in a better position to recognize than I am. These scenarios may seen like science fiction, but they can all be done with today's technology—and that technology is not expensive. The only requirement is that the work be done. The only shortage is the people to do the work.

If you don't work in one of the fields I use as an example, ask yourself the questions: "How could I use these ideas in what I want to do with my life?" "How could the answers to these questions help me make progress in my occupation?" and "What combination of technology would help me to design a new future in my profession?"

We have careers, organizations, families or other goals that consume our time. In some areas, computers have already had substantial impact. But many areas are new territory, just waiting for the proper talent and vision to bring the future together. Let's take a look at some possibilities.

Entertainment

Cathy has a dilemma. Logically, she sees that Lloyd has probably murdered Smithy, but when talking to Lloyd he seems so honest, truthful and good looking. Cathy doesn't want to believe that Lloyd is the guilty party. She would much prefer it if she could prove that Cliff was the perpetrator of the crime, but she needs more evidence. Cliff is so arrogant and full of himself. Cathy's confusion isn't helping any. If she doesn't move on with her investigation, Bill or Arnold may solve the mystery before her. Cathy enters a spine-tingling secret passage behind a bookcase and finds stairs leading down. She can hear running water in the distance which grows louder as she travels down into the semi-darkness. A cold chill runs through her body.

"Break time! The game's saved. Let's get a sandwich." The three players rise from their seats, leaving their computers frozen, and head for the kitchen. They were playing the latest interactive sleuth game. Their computers are attached via a local area network and are simultaneously playing the same game. The game is on a video disk that provides each player with the appropriate scenes and sound. They are playing in the individual mode where they work against each other to solve the crime. They can conceal evidence that they discover or leave false clues for the other detectives, but if caught they will encounter severe penalties. They interview witnesses who respond with digitized voices.

There are more than 100 possible scenarios included with the game, and there's even a mode where the detectives can work as teams, sharing information. In the next century, this game has become popular in both homes and the computer team arcades, where people play collaborative games of Swordmaster, Mysterious Crimes and Sea Battle.

*   *   *

Today, the entertainment industry is already a major investor in computer technology. We take for granted the computer-generated graphics in films that provide special effects unknown a decade ago. Our children (and a few of us parents) are addicted to video games, only coming up for an occasional bag of chips. The industry promises more interactive games with better animation and graphics. Our games will talk to us; possibly respond to our voices. Interactive technology, computers responding to the input of the user, is on the industry's collective mind, as well it should be. (Interactive concepts are discussed in more detail in Chapter Four "New Ways of Looking at Old Problems.") The '90s may well be called the interactive decade. By using video disk technology that can switch video clips according to the players' movements, we'll even have interactive video games in which the plot changes according to the viewers' decisions.

For the past 70 years, entertainment has been one-on-one: one listener locked into the broadcast of a local radio station, one viewer captivated by the latest television miniseries, one video game player in mortal combat with the computer.

The '90s could be the time for collaboration to come to entertainment: Teams of people using computers over a local area network, creating a fantastic group adventure, playing against either the computer or another team of players. For the first time we could have competitive computer team sports. The key word here is *collaboration*, but how would the concept of *mobility* or *artificial intelligence* affect entertainment and technology?

Education

Richard is in the sixth grade. He's anxious to go to school. Sometimes his parents worry about him because he often seems to prefer school over playing outside. This is a common problem for parents. In the '80s it was video games. Now, in the 21st century, it's school.

Part of the problem is that Richard is never really away from school. At any time, he can sit down at his computer and consult with the school computers and his friends from school via telephone lines. On occasion, he has been implicated in some school computer mischief. It's true that he and his classmates are learning at much faster rates than those measured by any previous standard, but sometimes it seems that they are learning too much. And they like it too much.

In the 21st century, the education system has transformed from a system of teaching to a system of collaboration. Students don't learn facts, they assimilate them as part of their knowledge and experience base. They don't have to memorize information any more than a twelve-year old boy must study to remember the goal he scored in yesterday's soccer game. Computer technology and some visionary educators are responsible for this change.

Looking back from the year 2000, we see that in the late 1980s and early 1990s, many teachers (then considered radical elements) recognized that computer technology was not being applied to education in the most productive manner. Rather than using the strengths of computers and associated systems, the schools were merely trying to parrot the efforts of the teachers.

The first educational programs were boring and soon lost the students' interest. The best teachers had always entertained the students while they learned, so the next improvement was adding video game entertainment to the educational software. This was a great improvement for the students, yet the visionary educators realized that this approach was still not taking advantage of the power of computer technology.

The education system was overburdened. Many computers sat unused in the classroom because the teacher was intimidated by the machine. The demands on the teachers were growing, and the old methods seemed entirely inadequate to the times. There was a shortage of truly good teachers, and it appeared that the shortage would get worse since there were less young people overall entering the work force. There were too few people entering the education profession. It seemed the situation would be dire by the year 2000.

At that time, a few daring and adventurous educators took the view that the entire approach to education must be re-thought—as if there were no school system at all. A new design would be created from the ground up. It was assumed that computer technology would have to be used productively because there would still be a shortage of well-qualified teachers. It was also accepted that the government would do little to help, since the government was an institution of status quo and not an instrument for creating a new future. These forward-thinking educators understood that their associates in the educational system would feel threatened by their efforts. New ways of thinking were required.

The first problem they tackled was the shortage of qualified teachers. They understood that the productive capacity of the best instructors must be increased through the better use of technology. The truly exceptional teachers must be able to reach more students while spending more time with the pupils who need the most help.

The next goal was to create an educational environment that was so stimulating that the students would look forward to Monday morning. Not just the best students, but every one of them.

The teachers' speculations transformed the role of the pupil from student to collaborator. The technology of local areas networks was used to connect all the students' computers. The instructor acted as a server, facilitator and inspiration for education. Software was designed to take advantage of the network technology. Students interacted with each other over the computer system, the sharper students assisting the slower students. They pulled their classmates along in a stimulating, interactive environment. The sharper students learned even more as they aided the slower students. The computer posed the problems and scenarios, the students posed questions and researched answers. The teachers monitored progress and offered special assistance as necessary. The teacher was now a facilitator, easily dealing with a hundred or more students. This was possible only because the student was no longer the problem of education, but part of the solution, aiding others at every turn. The technology and software systems designed by some very forward-looking educators made it all possible.

*   *   *

This is just one small glimpse of a possible future for education. It doesn't even explore other possibilities such as tying these school systems to the computers at home via modems or fiber optics. The University of Maine has already responded to the changing times. Many of Maine's potential college students are well beyond the commuting range of any universities, yet they are enrolled and attend classes via video hookups. Professors teach classes that are transmitted to remote locations around the state, giving people who otherwise would be forced to forego an education an opportunity to earn credits toward a degree.

The situation in Maine is not an isolated incident. It is a sample of a growing trend. Education has become a life-long process, and as the baby boomers in their 30s and 40s change direction in their lives, they will be looking for the tools to make those transitions. They won't be going to the colleges; the colleges will be coming to them. Computer technology will be a critical part of this transition, as remote adult education becomes one of the fastest-growing facets of our educational system.

Social Work

The year is 2010. Sally works in an older section of New York. Her primary job is to help the less advantaged improve their situation. The political mood has changed in the country. It has become accepted that the welfare programs of the '60s and '70s contributed to societal problems by robbing the recipients of their opportunity to build self-esteem. Sally's mandate is to give people the tools to rebuild their self-worth and their neighborhoods. Computers are now an integral part of those tools.

Sally carries a PenPad-type computer with her on all her calls. The computer maintains a digital cellular hookup to the main computers in the office. While she is working with her clients and assisting them with their future planning, she uses the computer as if it were a clipboard with enormous resources. Many of her clients own computers that were subsidized by the state via low-interest loans. They have received the proper training and now work for various companies doing computer work. This has made it possible for them to become self-supporting while maintaining their families at home. The children are able to enrich their education with the same computer hookup to the local school. It has generally been conceded that the funds spent to subsidize the computer social programs have been well worth it—providing a return to society, rather than increasing the problem through enforced dependency.

*   *   *

Of course, this computer scenario is simplistic. However, it illustrates a possibility. Computers are tools of independence, and are very flexible tools of productivity—they can be adapted to some of the most unusual circumstances. The technology is inexpensive and the new hardware triggers are greatly expanding the possibilities. Yet, today, who is considering the idea of helping people become self-sufficient through the innovative use of computer technology?

Crime Prevention and Solving

Bill routinely writes down the license numbers of strange vehicles located on his street. His neighborhood watch has assigned him this duty. It is a function that he performs whenever he sees a car he doesn't recognize. There is a network of neighborhood watch organizations throughout the city, each with a desktop computer tied via modem to the central neighborhood watch server computer. After Bill enters the license numbers they are forwarded to the server computer via modem. Bill and other neighbors also collect information about strangers sighted in the neighborhood or vehicles speeding by. Again, all of this is collected by the central server computer.

This city-wide neighborhood watch computer system is not part of the police department. Rather, it is a privately funded system set up by the local neighborhood. The police do get information from the system if a crime is committed, but all the work is done by private citizens. Anyone who owns a computer and a modem can act as a witness for the system as long as they supply their real name and address. The system has not only helped the police solve numerous crimes, but there has also been a dramatic drop in the crime rate since its implementation.

In the solving of crimes, the information in the system has actually been able to track suspects to and from the scene, whether they were walking or in a vehicle. When a crime is committed, the first step is for the police to request a correlation report from the watch organization. The police supply the location and time of the crime and the computer system will supply inbound traffic leading up to the crime scene before that time, and later outbound traffic leaving the crime scene. In some cases, based upon the outbound tracking, the police have arrived at the perpetrators' home prior to the lawbreaker. This information is supplied to the police only when a crime is committed, maintaining the privacy of law-abiding citizens.

The crime rate has dropped dramatically because the neighborhood watch computer system has made it almost impossible to escape undetected. Some private individuals have even mounted video cameras activated by motion detectors that record all passing traffic for late night surveillance. The average citizen feels much safer, but the criminals feel persecuted—and often they are.

* * *

In 19th century England, the London police routinely recorded the licenses of cabs passing in the night, noting the time and date. Often, crimes were solved by the mere fact that traffic could be tracked at night, when most crimes occurred. In this new age, "Little Brother" is watching, as pointed out by the previously mentioned Rodney King incident in Los Angeles. The power of technology can be in everyone's hands. With the aid of computers, many new crime prevention and solving tools will be developed. Better systems for reporting crimes while gathering and analyzing evidence will be available. People may routinely report incidents via modem, alerting both the police and the neighbors. Home security may be controlled and monitored by the household computer. The computer opportunities are waiting to be seized.

Environmental Issues

The number of people telecommuting has dramatically increased. Even though there are now economical electric cars for getting to and from work, many telecommute two or three days a week. Employees can log-on at work via modem, or, as is the case with the larger companies, a fiber-optic connection. They are able to directly collaborate and conference with their associates either with the typed word or a video hookup. Some employees even live hundreds of miles from their companies.

It began in the late 1980s and accelerated through the 1990s. People started to move away from the major population centers. Fed up with the traffic and crime, people moved to the locations they loved most. While many headed for the sunbelt, even more relocated to the mountains and remote coastal areas. The computer had made it possible for people to live where they wanted and continue to be employed by the same company. Rather than people moving to new jobs around the country, the new jobs moved to the people. Mobility had taken on new meaning.

As a result, pollution took a dramatic drop in the cities, making the quality of life much better for those who chose to stay. As the world economy continued to shift away from an industrial base to a service and information base, the environment had become a major beneficiary. The use of computers and the building of better nuclear power plants had contributed to the decline of oil burning, further contributing to the improved situation. The demand for paper had declined with most local newspapers publishing via computer media. As a result, there was less demand for pulp—and most of that was supplied through recycling.

*   *   *

This is merely a hypothetical year 2010, offering possibilities for today. Many environmentalists feel that technology is the root of our environmental problems. To the contrary, the benefits of technology—computer technology in particular—can provide us with the means to clean up our own waste. Rather than calling for a movement back to nature, time could be better spent promoting the use of new technology in ways that will decrease the destruction of the environment. Whether technology will be the problem of the future or the solution will be up to us.

Media

It amazes Jim how much things have changed. He still reads the newspaper every morning, but now he reads it without the paper. He still drinks his coffee and eats his breakfast while he's reading the news, but now he doesn't get up from the table with ink-stained fingers. Much more importantly, his news is tailored for him. Jim has registered with his news service the topics and subjects that interest him most. Each morning the headlines he reviews are those that are most relevant to him. Jim can still search for all the other news, but he doesn't have to search for *his* news. Jim's newspaper comes in a tablet computer, and he uses a pen to turn the electronic pages. He never thought the day would come that he would give up the old reliable paper newspaper, but now the desire for convenience, accuracy, and news tailoring has brought the electronic newspaper.

The tablet computer goes with him anywhere. When he first bought the machine, it didn't occur to him that he would be using it to read the news. As a manufacturer's representative, Jim's purpose in buying the computer was business. But now a new world of information has been opened to him. He can read his electronic newspaper anywhere, even in bed.

Jim's news system does more than just give him the news. His newspaper is tailored for him. Based on Jim's input, each day the computer highlights the news that is most relevant to Jim and his work. As news stories are filed at the news organizations, the main computers sort and channel them to the people who have indicated their particular interests. Of course, everyone gets the major stories, but on a number of occasions Jim has been able to stay one step ahead in his business by knowing some obscure—yet relevant—business event. And Jim isn't forced to search numerous publications to find his news.

Jim subscribes to one of the major networks. In the early 1990s, only the seeds of these now massive networks existed. The news was delivered through television, radio, paper newspapers and a few computer information systems. Most of the news was limited to major events, whether on the world or local level. It was time-consuming. If you watched television, news was parceled out in short segments.

Entertaining though they were, they rarely contained much substance. The radio offered the same kind of service, though it was used primarily while commuting in an automobile. The newspaper gave much more in-depth information on the topic, but still the reader had no choice as to what the topic would be. Primitive entertainment was the best description for the media of the 1990s.

At that time, there existed services that supplied news and other information directly to computers in offices and homes. They could be called the forerunners of the modern electronic newspaper. Yet these were not the companies that revolutionized media. The heros in this revolution were individual entrepreneurs, often working out of the homes. They were the ones who brought living information to the fingertips, or pentips, of the average person. They each started as one person trying to get one job done, and they evolved into huge thinking networks of information and knowledge. The major corporations of the time never saw it coming. The rapid growth of modems attached to home computers in the 1990s triggered the new media industries that provided news, entertainment, travel information, weather, buying services and much more.

One person started a computer system that would offer local sports news 24-hours a day. It was supported by local sporting goods dealers whose ads were displayed on the system. Another person started an on-line system that supplied travel information supported by the local travel industry. As these independent systems began to proliferate, they formed networks with complementary systems. These networks eventually became the dominant source of information for business and family use.

A classic example was Steve's Around Town system. In 1992, Steve was 39 years old and looking at no further advancement at General Corporation. He was frustrated and disappointed with his career. His only pleasures were his family and his hobby of working on his computer at home. He had become very accomplished on the computer, and would tinker with his system almost every night. His other entertainment was taking the family out to dinner once a week.

These family trips to restaurants were a welcome break for everyone. They loved the adventure of trying new and different eating establishments. The problem was locating those new and different restaurants. It was difficult to get any information about the restaurants other than name and address. Steve felt it would be great if there were somewhere he could call with his computer to read the entire menu, including specials. Steve took it upon himself to create such a system.

Steve started by creating a database of all the restaurants in his area. He categorized them by their location and the type of food they served. As he would visit each restaurant with his family he would write a short description of the establishment. Steve set up a computer, modem and phone line dedicated to providing this information to anyone who called. He left messages on local electronic bulletin board systems letting people know they could call for this free information. Soon, Steve's Around Town was getting hundreds of phone calls a day. The primary advantage to the system was that callers could quickly isolate their choices by location and type of cuisine.

As restaurants became aware of Steve's system, they inquired about putting extra information, like weekly specials, on the system. For a small fee, Steve offered this service. He was soon earning a small supplement to his income plus paying for the system itself.

Steve's system became known as *the* way to find a restaurant in his hometown. It was soon connected to a local area network capable of handling thousands of phone calls a day. It was all financed by the restaurants who purchased space on his system. Some even offered their complete menu via Steve's system. In the mid-1990s, Steve put his listings in a voice mail system that could be accessed by any telephone. Ultimately, Steve connected with other similar systems around the country, creating a huge network of independent small businesses. National food and entertainment companies would purchase space on the entire national network, increasing the revenues for all of the independent members.

Early on, Steve was able to quit his job and pursue his new business full-time. The importance of Steve's business was not his idea—thousands of others had similar ideas. What was important was his application of technology to an old problem. He was doing it, while many others were talking about it.

As it turned out, many other people were operating similar systems with varying degrees of success. Some concentrated on sports, others worked with the arts, and still others took a particular political bent. Some sold their service; others received their income through advertising. By the year 2000, many of these entrepreneurs were tying their systems together, offering each of the subscribers more features. Eventually, these networks produced innovations like "The Living Yellow Pages," which offer full multimedia looks at local businesses. A subscriber could actually watch videos of the retailer's operations and special offers. The push of a button would hook the subscriber's computer directly to the retailer.

Jim, our manufacturer's representative, was a subscriber to one of these networks. The network offerings were almost unlimited because the subscribers were also collaborators and resources for the network. The network had become Jim's primary resource for the daily news.

* * *

In the next decade, the modem is the likely trigger for on-line services, many of them free and supported by advertising. Convenience and tailoring are the consumer demands that will change how we interact with the media. The videotape recorder has already severely cut into television revenues. As more viewers rent films to watch at their convenience, the value of television advertising drops. Even recording commercial television shows for later viewing destroys the value of advertising, as VCR owners zip by the commercial messages in the "fast-forward" mode. How businesses advertise will change in the future as reaching the market becomes more difficult. But the special search and retrieval functions of the computer will make sales easier to the customers who know what they want to buy.

Health and Medicine

Joan finally felt good about a computer taking up space in her house. It was adding a new level of security to her life. She felt that the computer was doing a great job of keeping her kids healthy. Some of the worries of motherhood were now easier to bear. Joan's computer included a software package called *HouseCall*.

HouseCall was relatively simple. It was a diskette similar to a Compact Disc (CD). In fact, it was called a CD-ROM (Compact Disc– Read-Only Memory). She had actually purchased the system from the local medical society and it ran on the CD-ROM drive attached to her computer. The beauty of the system was that late at night, which was the only time her kids would get sick, she could get a safe diagnosis of the situation without calling the doctor. (The doctor loved it.)

The Medical Association had brought together a team of medical experts and created the diagnostic system to be used at home. It was simple to use and contained, literally, the knowledge of numerous medical experts. Joan would take her child's temperature, note clamminess and other symptoms, then answer the questions that the computer supplied. If Joan didn't understand a question, the computer would run a video demonstrating and explaining the terminology. In many cases, the computer advised her that most probably her child was infected by a 24-hour virus, but to continue to check for symptoms after bringing down his temperature with a non-aspirin pain-reliever. When it was appropriate, the computer would instruct Joan to call the doctor or take the child directly to the hospital. On one occasion, Joan had saved one of her guests by quickly diagnosing, via *HouseCall,* the symptoms of a heart attack and rushing him to the hospital. He'd thought he had indigestion.

The computer system was widely used in medical school as interactive instruction for medical students. It was considered good medical practice for doctors to run their patients' symptoms through the system to check for less-common illnesses that might match the symptoms. Many lives had been saved with this cross-check of the M.D.'s work.

*   *   *

The technology and expertise needed to create this type of expert medical system is available today. Quite possibly, someone has already developed one, though concerns about liability might limit its availability to the general market.

Computers are being used in almost every aspect of medicine, but there are many more applications that could have general market appeal waiting to be exploited. A doctor could dispense medical advice to regular customers via modem. Different sets of pre-written medical instructions could be relayed to a patient's computer, depending on the nature of the complaint. A computer-based referral service could be available for patients who need to see a specialist or get a second opinion. Forums for doctors who are looking for specific new cures could be constructed. The opportunities are only limited by the number of problems.

Only the Beginning

This chapter does not cover all walks of life, nor should it. Politics, the military, engineering, science and many other fields all have new areas of opportunity opening as a result of new technologies acting as hardware triggers. There are enough examples here from diverse occupations to allow you to start your own fantasizing. This is just the beginning. To create new visions, we need new ways of looking at old problems. With new visions and technology tools, we can create new ways of doing things. As we work through the concepts in the next chapter, many more opportunities will spring forth.

Chapter Four
New Ways of Looking at Old Problems

"The essence of the creative act is to see the familiar as strange."

— Anonymous

The emphasis of the book *Future Perfect* was new ways of looking at old problems. Over the centuries, we have come to take the same rote approach to almost all our endeavors. The classroom operates in essentially the same manner as it did 100 years ago. Hospitals have evolved little in their organization or approach to healing. Government procedures are based on systems that were ideal for past centuries, but have become increasingly inadequate for today. The most common explanation is, "We've always done it that way." Even computer technology tends to be applied in the same old ways. We try to model human activity rather than looking for new ways to solve problems.

We can't afford the luxury of accepting past approaches as the solutions for the future—especially while the new tools of technology are giving us incredible new opportunities. When applying computer technology to education, it is commonly thought that the best use of computers is to computerize the teaching method of Mrs. Smith, the exceptionally talented seventh-grade Social Studies teacher, or that of other talented instructors. It's naturally assumed that all we need is more of what was so good in the past. The primary emphasis of almost all computer applications has been to do more, faster.

Over the last decade, we have taken the old solutions and computerized them. We get many more answers per second, but we haven't spent much time questioning our methods.

The entrepreneurs of the future will be taking another point of view; one that would never dawn on most of us. When we see their new innovations, we'll slap our heads and say, "Wow! I wish I'd thought of that." These developments will look so simple, yet undeniably clever.

For example, when we think of Fred, the traveling executive, our first thought is to get him more information while he's on the road. We build him a computer that he can take with him. We get him a modem that he can plug into a hotel phone. We ensure that he has everything he needs for mobility. Mobility is the key concept. Traditionally, we have created mobility by building smaller, easier-to-move equipment, but that's just one side of the coin.

Let's take another viewpoint: Traveling is an extraordinary waste of human time. It's exhausting and tedious. If we view the problem of mobility as one of moving information and not one of moving human bodies, an entirely new approach starts to evolve. The question is now, "How do we get the work to the person?" not "How do we get the person to the work?"

Jobs can be redesigned. Video conferencing from remote areas is a possibility. In the words of Davis, "anytime, anyplace." We are able to function regardless of our location or the time of day. Systems of collaboration will be built, helping us acquire a new freedom: the freedom *from* travel. The concept becomes mobility of information rather than mobility of people.

We think of computers as primarily tools for business and industry. We consider them instruments for productivity, not vehicles for social change. Most predictions for the future of computers embrace doing more, faster. Rarely do we envision computers offering different, better solutions. Yet computers are most certainly tools for making things both different and better with their own unique strengths. That's where the greatest opportunities lie: using computer strengths to create not necessarily faster tools, but better tools.

Productivity

Traditionally, computers have been tools of productivity. The essence of productivity is to obtain increased results, whether by doing more or wasting less. The only way that businesses and people can earn more without the accompanying destruction of earnings called inflation is to become more productive: do more with less. If more value is added to a product or service without an increase in cost, that's an increase in productivity. A vast number of future computer opportunities will be through increased productivity. The Video Toaster can turn an Amiga computer into a professional video editing studio at a fraction of the cost of a Hollywood studio. This is a traditional increase in productivity.

The computer increases productivity by saving time and decreasing errors. Computers can perform many functions thousands of times faster than humans. This has provided huge gains where the primary obstacle to productivity was human slowness. The computer also is many times more accurate and reliable than the human. This has further increased productivity by building a product or service with more dependable elements. Ninety-nine percent of today's computer productivity applications emphasize the elements of speed and accuracy. While these computer strengths will continue to play a major role in the computer opportunities of the next decade, many new computer industries will be the offspring of other productivity factors such as collaboration, mobility, interaction, specialization, generalization and creativity.

This chapter is concerned with these other issues of productivity; here we will explore many truly innovative computer opportunities.

Collaboration

Historically, quantum leaps in human achievement are recorded as the acts of a few talented individuals. Yet when we research the times and events that produced our heros, we find that their achievements were the offspring of the thoughts, words and actions of many others who came before them. Just as Socrates taught Plato and Plato tutored Aristotle, there were many other Greek philosophers who preceded them. Beethoven and Mozart were carrying on the work of an epoch heavily influenced by Bach. The artist Raphael studied under the influence of Leonardo da Vinci and Michelangelo. Tycho, the astronomical observer, collaborated with Kepler, the theorist. Throughout history, all the great periods of leadership were continuous lines of individuals collaborating to create a climate for the breakthroughs achieved by the genius of an Aristotle, a Mozart, a Newton or an Einstein. Though on the surface it appears to be the brilliant work of one person, the new discoveries would not have occurred without the contributions of the numerous lesser minds that set the stage and created the climate. History forgets their names, but without them there would not have been the great opportunities for achievement.

Collaboration continues to be one of the keys to human success. There are few people—if any—who can see it all, do it all and teach it all. We build on our own strengths and the strengths of others. A small group of people working in a team can make individual weaknesses irrelevant by substituting one person's talent for another's deficiency. Creativity is sparked by the exchange of ideas.

This is the basis of scientific development. A picture is often painted of the lone scientist working 20 hours a day in a basement laboratory, edging toward a major breakthrough. The history books rarely write about the years of study under a particularly influential professor, or the inspiration of colleagues, or the scientific correspondence and conferences that may have redirected the efforts of our hero. Most progress in science and technology is made in a leapfrog fashion, with each new advance coming on the back of a previous advance which came off the back of another—and still another.

Collaboration is one of the key issues for today's technology. How do we use computers to bring together the great ideas necessary for progress? What are the tools that will help us inspire and stimulate achievement through interaction? How do we apply these tools to the problems of today?

In our day-to-day life we have moved away from collaboration toward isolation. Our entertainment is between the individual and the screen, whether television or computer. Our educational system is a relationship between the student and the teacher. Our health system is geared toward doctor-patient interaction. In the workplace, the primary concern has been the manager-subordinate relationship. These are the signs of mediocrity, not human achievement.

The essence of collaboration is widely shared information. The greater the dissemination of information, the greater the potential for achievement. The future tools of collaboration are available today.

Local area networks tie groups of computers together, making the sharing of information organized and easy. Laser disk technology allows the accumulation and dissemination of huge databases of knowledge for sharing with colleagues. Modems and other data transmission technologies offer the transfer and sharing of information over great geographic distances.

These are the tools—here today—that make greater collaboration possible. How does it work?

*   *   *

In the future of education, students become collaborators as well as pupils. (This is the model for post graduate education at most universities.) Their mission is not merely to learn, but to contribute. As they work on the classroom computer network under the guidance of their instructor, they contribute to the class database, helping some students while learning from the expertise of others. The programming of the computer network system (designed by a collaboration of educators dedicated to optimizing the use of computers in education) guides the class objectives.

*   *   *

In politics, a few conscientious members of Congress set up computer systems to take on-line calls from constituents. Voters can call with their computer and modem to get the views of the congress person, as well as leave their own opinions. As issues develop and change, the Congress members get almost instant feedback on their performance.

Of course, many members of Congress may not want this level of direct accountability to the people, yet this form of collaboration would cut into the influence of special interest groups, especially if voters could leave political contributions while on-line.

Thinking in terms of collaboration gives new insight into most walks of life. Many of the old one-on-one ways of doing business have seemed more expedient. It takes less time to work with only one person at a time. But today, with the use of computer technology, it is possible to get beneficial, organized collaboration without the overwhelming consumption of time. Here is a possibility:

*   *   *

Remote Brainstorming: Hooked via modems to a server with controlling software, a group of engineers located around the world participate in an idea-generating session. They are all addressing a specific engineering problem. The controlling software takes the groups through the steps of problem definition, alternative generating and action planning, while the participants input their ideas continuously and review those of others. The procedure is found to be so powerful and fast that it is adapted to group situations on local area networks. The process of remote brainstorming is like having everyone talk at the same time, yet it makes complete, organized sense. It's a synergy that sparks creativity and solves problems. When done with anonymity, even the reluctant tend to be forceful. Future computing systems that can handle pictures and charts in addition to today's text-based systems will make physical presence in a brainstorming session totally irrelevant.

*   *   *

Collaboration is two or more people working toward the same goal simultaneously. With modems, networks and mass storage devices, computer systems can be designed to act as human collaboration tools. Not only will the collaboration be faster, but it will also be more productive.

Mobility

Anytime, anyplace. The future moves toward a state where time and geography are no longer treated as limitations, but as resources.

In the 1980s, computers became such an important part of doing business that it soon became imperative that the business person have access to a computer anytime, anywhere. Mobility became the watchword, and into the picture came the portable computer. First came the "luggables"; the size and weight of a small suitcase—not even fitting under the seat in an airplane. Then we were given laptop computers. Being much more convenient, business people were soon replacing their briefcases with laptops. Computers continued to shrink until they became so small that it was impossible for most people to use the keyboard without finger cramps. In the 1990s, PenPad-type computers will displace the laptop as the computer of choice for the mobile professional. (See Chapter Five, "Hardware Triggers.")

But the concept of mobility is not limited to carrying technology with you. After all, technology is only a tool; it's the result that's important. Computers are tools of information, and information delivery is the crucial issue.

Mobility does not necessarily mean traveling anywhere. It could mean staying home. Mobility is the ability to act without regard to time or geography. It could mean staying put rather than going to the office. Mobility may entail working at two o'clock in the morning. Mobility may imply attending an international conference in London without ever leaving your office. Mobility is more than carrying a computer on a trip. After all, it isn't the mobility of the computer that is important, it's the mobility of the work. Mobility is the ability to accomplish a task anytime, anyplace. To free ourselves for greater productivity, we must rid ourselves of the notion that mobile technology necessarily implies carrying a computer.

*   *   *

Artificial travel: Through the use of video hookups, students are able to travel through modern-day Greece, viewing the ruins. Simulations of Ancient Greece fill in the historical gaps, giving new meaning to history class.

*   *   *

In the 1990s, more tools will be developed to eliminate the need for travel. Higher-speed modems will be available for communications, acting as a stopgap until the day the world is networked with fiber optic cables. Fax and voice mail technology will continue to be rapid-growth industries.

When it's necessary to be truly mobile, digital cellular systems will be used to send information directly to the computer on location. A paging company already exists that offers data transfer services to palmtop computers in the field. Infrared connections are used for the new PocketPhones. At certain geographic locations, micro cellular technology will allow shirt pocket phones to work almost anywhere.

The concept of mobility is the basis for many of the new computer industries in the 1990s. Whether the traveler is carrying the information or the information is carried to the computer, all of life's endeavors will enjoy greater freedom of movement.

Interactive

In the 1960s and 1970s, parents worried about the fact that children spent six hours a day in front of the television. They knew their kids were turning into vegetables, eventually doomed to become couch potatoes. Some children did grow up to be couch potatoes, running to the video store every weekend while stocking up on their favorite beer and chips. The only reason more people didn't give in to the box is that they became bored. The continual drone of the television with the incessant blaring of "important messages" drove most to seek relief elsewhere.

Today, there is an even more insidious addiction affecting our youth. It's called the video game and has caused even the youngest children to abandon Saturday morning cartoons. Video games are far worse than television because there is no limit to how often or how long the child will be consumed. If the parent says, "It's time to go to bed," the child responds, "Just wait until I get killed." Two hours later the young arcadist is still at it.

Many parents appreciate the babysitting effect of these games. But unless you have an only child, the fighting that ensues from kids "trying to share" is unbearable. What is this evil that has entered our homes? How does it hold our children to a point where the former household god, the television, is relegated to the position of mild amusement?

The key word is "interactive." The video game is interactive. It responds to the thoughts, movements and emotions of the player. The television just sits and blares, not caring about the feelings and motives of the viewer. If the viewer leaves the room the television goes on, knowing there is always another fool somewhere who is watching. The video game, however, waits for the master to return before starting off with the adventure again. If you push the stick in one direction the character will jump; in another direction the screen image ducks. The video game involves all the senses except taste and smell. The player is totally involved. Any rational society would ban interactive video games. Luckily, we are not in a rational society.

Interaction is one of the most effective concepts for maintaining the attention of a human. It gives power to the individual. Decisions can be implemented immediately. Tests can be made with instantaneous results. The direct response of interaction captivates the subjects and urges them to try more. The bells and whistles of video games may entertain, but it's the interaction that hypnotizes. One of the key concepts for the computer industries of the 1990s is interaction.

The entertainment industry has taken the lead in interactive technology, using it extensively in arcade and adventure games, but many of the best applications will be in education. I have witnessed a child's book on a CD-ROM disk and Macintosh computer that reads itself to the child. If the child uses the mouse to click on a ball in the picture, the computer displays the word, "ball," then pronounces it. As the computer reads through the book, it highlights the words that are being read. If desired, the computer will even translate a highlighted word into another language, like Spanish. These types of interactive industries will explode into the next century and beyond. Many of the new applications are easy to envision.

* * *

Laser disk videos will be available that respond to input from one or more viewers. As the viewers are watching a mystery, they have options to select at key points. Depending on their selection, the laser disk will jump to another sequence of the mystery, with alternate outcomes depending on the decisions of the viewers. Interactive video is already in the works.

* * *

Investment by the entertainment industry will develop much of the interactive technology, but there are many other occupations that will benefit from it.

* * *

In the area of health, interactive exercise equipment will be available that allows you to compete against real athletes on video. The equipment provides the forces required to simulate both the game and the necessary reactions. The Wimbledon Tennis Video Interexerciser could be very popular, but the Mike Tyson Sparring machine may gather dust. Laser disk technology will be a primary ingredient of this type of system.

*   *   *

In politics, legislators could set up polling systems that would pose questions to the constituents via a modem and computer. The voters could respond directly to the question or comment on other issues directly to their representative's computer system. It has been found that people are much more likely to provide written response via a computer than by writing and posting a letter.

The possibilities for interactive systems being applied in our society are almost endless. The computer equipment necessary for these new industries is laser disk technology with its huge storage capacities, ease of data movement and ability to combine video, audio and data organization.

Specialization

Most people have found that success requires specialization. The general practitioner medical doctor has become a rare person. Most medical professionals have found it necessary to specialize—to become an expert in one particular area. This makes them more effective as a doctors, and when collaborating with others, the group has more knowledge than any one individual. Specialization is a continuing trend in the future. The demands of knowledge in most professions require us to narrow our focus.

Yet as we become more specialized, who will be the generalists who will call in the specialist? There must be someone who will keep the "big picture," guiding the actions of all the players. How can anyone have enough knowledge to be qualified to do this job in the future?

In the next decade, access to expert knowledge will be transferred to those who need it most. Libraries will be accumulated on laser disks that will help even the novice work through the most complicated problems. These systems are called expert systems. There will be medical systems, legal systems, engineering systems, business systems, etc., all dispensing expert services at the touch of a button. The vast data libraries now available on CD-ROM are the forerunners of expert systems. They are available today, and their growth will continue into the year 2000. New companies will emerge, each specializing in a type of expertise.

"Expert Systems" will be a watchword of the '90s. An expert computer system is a database of specialized information that provides a user with the same knowledge and expertise as a specialist in that area. As more databases with built-in logical research and diagnosing software become available, the average computer user will have a increasing number of experts at his or her fingertips. These expert systems will give the consumer advice and guidance equal to that of a consultant in the area, only at a much lower cost.

These expert systems will not come about without controversy. Many professional groups will attempt to outlaw the expert systems, fearing they could make the professional redundant. For example, the legal profession will fear the loss of consultation fees if legal systems come into widespread use. No doubt there will be attempts to ban such systems by passing legislation, all in the name of protecting the individual. Eventually, the systems will be accepted by all as a normal and new way of doing business, freeing up the true professional for the important work of the future.

In the business world, specialization is called "niche marketing." Specializing in one small corner of a market has provided prosperity for many companies. In publishing it is common for one publisher to specialize in medical books while another may only address the textbook market. Some computer dealers may specialize in desktop publishing solutions, while others offer only local area network services. Specialization works because it is possible to concentrate resources and do well in one small area, whereas addressing too large a market will dilute efforts, creating mediocrity.

Computers make specialization easier. They help to gather knowledge in the area of specialization. They assist in the organization of knowledge, making presentation of data in a logical manner much more powerful. It is the specialization of the computer that creates new industries.

The narrow application of laser printers to the graphics and printing industry created desktop publishing. The computers for desktop publishing were not purchased for their general business capabilities, though they were very capable accounting and administration vehicles, but rather for their graphics and display capabilities. Those desktop publishing computers tend to be used almost exclusively for desktop publishing. There are other computers to help administer the business. A new industry was created by using the computer to specialize in one area. Just as the laser printer combined with the computer created the desktop publishing industry, most of the new computer businesses in the '90s will be the product of specialization. The general markets like word processing and database management have been saturated with mature businesses who did their growing in the '80s. The new industries will be subsets of the older industries, just as accounting is a subset of database management.

The question is not *if* you should specialize, but *how* you should specialize. In our new society of fragmented-yet-networked organizations, each part will do what it does best. Thinking in terms of specialization is important for the application of technology into the next century.

General Products Specialized

As I was walking through a local retail store, I noticed a group of people crowded around a booth. I managed to peek through the crowd and get a closer look at what was causing all the commotion. It was children's books. For the most part these books were much like any other children's books, but with one important exception: Each book was being personalized for the customer. A child's name could be inserted via computer into the text of the story, then be printed and bound on the spot. It was the customization of a mass product.

Mass customization is the creation of a specialized product from generalized ingredients. In other words, we continue to get the advantages of mass production while offering an individualized product. The computer is the tool of mass customization. Without it, the concept and reality would be severely limited.

Today, people want the personalized products, but the cost of customizing outside of certain limitations is prohibitive. The computer is changing this in most industries. Computers are capable of both mass producing and customizing simultaneously, automatically making the changes in the assembly line.

When buying computers, people are already the beneficiaries of mass customization. The new buyer tells the dealer which capabilities are desired, and the dealer customizes the machine—often on the spot. In the next decade more businesses will be moving toward the individualization of products at the retail level. The consumers are demanding this level of service, and the computer can deliver it.

In his book, *Microcosm*, George Gilder points out that even the microchips that make up the inner workings and hidden mechanisms of a computer are moving toward mass customization. Silicon compilers, which design chips from engineering requirements and new manufacturing techniques, are making it relatively inexpensive to build new chip sets, even in small quantities. This may give us more specialized hardware in smaller—yet affordable—quantities in the next century.

Rather than people buying general-purpose computers like the PC, Mac, or workstation, each computer—including the chips—could be delivered according to customer specifications.

This type of mass customization of computer chips could create a new era of inventors. Individuals could afford to design and produce, in small quantities, devices for almost every walk of life. Niche markets would be available for specialized, tailored security or communications devices. The executive could order a custom computer with multiple processors, designed for specific problems. For those specific problems, that computer would do more, faster. Proprietary aspects of the application would be locked inside the hardware, eliminating today's problem of software piracy and work-alike ripoffs. Today, most tailoring must be done with software; in the next century it could be done with hardware.

Generalizing Details

Another strength of the computer is creating a "big picture" from numerous little details. In this manner, the computer can be a tool of discovery.

In 1971, I was taking a course in stellar astrophysics. The first couple of weeks we studied the measurement and calculation of stellar distances and such (light years, etc.). That portion of the course was fairly straightforward and not beyond my comprehension. Then we started the incomprehensible task of studying stellar evolution, or stars from birth to death. This turned out to be a terribly complicated problem. It was so complicated that at one point we were studying four different, competing theories, each with a formula as long as my arm. Each formula was attempting to describe the chaos of stellar evolution in a different manner. In the course of discussions, the professor indicated the correct method for solving problems was to calculate the results from each formula, add them together and divide by four.

At that point I closed the book, never to open it again. If the experts couldn't figure out which equation was right, I had the course sacked.

Little did I know that about that time a new approach to science and computers was emerging. People were starting to use computers to plot equations that seemed to behave chaotically. As computers became faster and more powerful, the computer plots became more detailed. The scientists began to notice that there were patterns forming in their plots. Maybe chaos wasn't chaotic after all. Simple equations that appeared to turn chaotic at certain stages displayed an overall, general pattern. The patterns were similar to those seen in weather formations. Solar flares seemed to match some of the other plots. Turbulence was modeled by still other sets of simple equations. What appeared to be meaningless noise when viewed as data became a beautiful, recognizable pattern when viewed as a whole. The implications are immense: It's like solving a two million piece jigsaw puzzle; the big picture emerges as the details are inserted. There is new hope for stellar astrophysics.

Chaos has become a new field of science and mathematics, attempting to find patterns in what was always considered unpredictable. Weather, economics, sociology and other similar disciplines have always been too complicated for traditional approaches to mathematics. The computer, with its relentless grinding power, gives us a tool for generalizing the specific. As we feed the details of our work into the computer, the software organizes and displays the data. As the process proceeds, we start to recognize patterns. Those patterns reflect probabilities. They could be probabilities of behavior or probabilities of weather.

If we were to plot the relocation of people worldwide, showing each person's move—whether across town or to another country— patterns of movement would emerge. Though the general trend of movement would tend to remain the same over periods of years, a change in that trend could be the preliminary sign of significant demographic shifts. If these changes were plotted, we would have a tool of prediction. What will be the new geographic growth areas? Will the declining population leave a location in a depression? What services will be needed to deal with both growing and declining areas?

*　　*　　*

A new computer field is emerging called desktop mapping. Database software is used to correlate information to maps. One company, MapInfo, has grown by providing both the geographically oriented database software and the map data on disk. This software will provide both details for specialization and generalized information for spotting trends.

*　　*　　*

Historically, when we see the trends of demographic shifts, we attempt to stop the trend. If people are leaving a community, we try to stop them. If people are entering another location rapidly, we pass no-growth legislation. But by the time we see the trend, it's too late to stop it, even if it were possible to arrest it at some earlier stage. If it isn't possible to stop what seem to be undesirable shifts, with computer-generalized details of movement changes it is at least possible to recognize the problems and take advantage of the opportunities created by these changes.

The concept of generalizing details helps us to identify trends, cycles and patterns. It is the rearrangement of details that gives new information. Just as a chart of monthly sales will help us predict our profits (or eventual demise), it is possible for details of consumer behavior to project future demographic shifts. The computer has the power to present a generalization of specifics. When applied to the appropriate endeavor, this could be a powerful tool.

Creativity

Computers themselves are not creative. Though work in artificial intelligence has helped computers do visual and sound recognition and analysis, there is nothing close to the power of the human mind for creativity. Creativity often seems to be the production of something out of nothing, but in real terms, even creativity has basic ingredients. The mark of creativity is not so much the ingredients of the composition as the way that it is composed. Computers may be both the tools and ingredients of creativity, but the work remains the domain of the human.

The computer can be a tremendous aid to creativity as a liberator. By taking much of the boring drudgery away from the human, the computer releases the human mind for creative functions. For example, when a writer lets the words pour without concern for the mechanics of spelling, correcting typographical errors and messing with bottles of correction fluid, the creative juices start to flow. The computer frees the mind for the work it does best: creating

The computer is also an excellent tool for stimulating creativity. The computer can mix and match traditional media and concepts in non-traditional ways to stimulate the human mind to new thoughts. The generalized plots of weather or economics can spark the human to new insights—insights that lead to new innovations and solutions.

Stimulation

When I was young my father and brother built a fishpond in the front yard. Stocked with Japanese Koi, it was an endless source of amusement. As it happened, there was a slow leak in the pond that caused the water level to be a little lower each day. I often wondered whether the slow leak and dropping water level caused concern for the fish. I would visualize myself as one of the fish and contemplate the situation.

While imagining myself floating underwater, I realized that as a fish I wasn't concerned one bit about the water level dropping: It was the rising of the ground that caused me concern. Each day the bottom of the pond was a little higher, and if it continued I would be pushed right out of the water. Luckily for me, from time to time a turbulence on the surface would push the bottom back down.

Does a fish see the surface of the water dropping or the bottom of the pond rising? It depends on its reference point. By changing that reference point we change our point of view, and therefore our outlook.

This is one way we can use a computer to stimulate creativity. Through the computer tools of multimedia we can create new views of life and problems, thereby stimulating new solutions. Every time I see a new piece of computer hardware, ideas for computer applications pop into my head. They all appear to be a trigger in some sense, though some have much stronger possibilities than others. On many different levels, computers can act as stimulators.

Visualization

As far as we know, humans are the only species that is aware of an impending end to its life. We know that someday each one of us will die. That is a unique awareness that implies other qualities. We have the ability to project a probable future. We can plan a possible future. We can visualize change. We can set goals. One of the primary seeds of creativity is the visualization of a goal. If we can see it, we can possibly create it.

Computers can help us create visualizations. The old business spreadsheet on the computer is a tool of visualization. We project what we feel will be the sales for the next year. Next, the costs are projected. The computer then calculates the probable profit (or loss). As we adjust numbers and play "What if?", the visualizations change. We make decisions today based on plans for tomorrow.

Adding laser disk technology and video graphics will create even more powerful, stimulating visualizations. A completed house will be viewed in three-dimensional form, the computer user strolling through it. A concerto will be tested in full orchestra before the first note is penned. A new medical technique will be perfected in an "artificial surgery" environment prior to ever being used on a live patient.

Strategy

Strategy is grand design. It is composed of the ruling principles that drive us toward our goals. It may be developed from inspiration or perspiration, but it is the master plan we create that governs all others. Strategy is the generalization of the specific details and tactics to come later.

The computer assists with strategy by accumulating details and organizing them in a fashion that allows the human mind to grasp the "big picture." The information becomes the catalyst for the development of strategy, stimulating the creativity necessary for building an effective design.

For example, the computer charts and graphs we use in business are snapshots of details presented in a general form. These glimpses into our business stimulate our strategies for the future. Either things appear to be on track or changes in strategy are necessary. Without this generalized picture, we may never recognize the need to shift strategy until it's too late. These same "big picture" approaches can be applied to national government policies and economics by using computers to generate the tools that display trends of details. Much more than a one-number index of economic changes, but a plot of numerous data points that give us the flow of the pattern and changes in the pattern. Creative strategy is then the fallout of having a better grasp on the situation.

These are the tools of human creativity. They can be called mind games or mental gymnastics, but the act of recombining logical thoughts in seemingly random order—then looking for new order—can stimulate the human mind to new sequences. The computer is a tool for relieving the brute-force work of the human mind, but more important, it is a tool for stimulation as it recombines the old into a new form. As equipment for stimulation, simulation and sparking strategy, the computer is extremely adept.

There are many ways to use the computer for creative purposes, whether for "remote brainstorming" or generalizing a "big picture" from details. These methods themselves are new computer opportunities, and the demand for creativity will increase in the next decade.

Human Limitations

Humans tend to be pretty flexible. They can adapt to most situations and take advantage of opportunities as they are presented.

But sometimes in the course of invention we tend to ask too much of people, and then wonder why the product didn't sell. There are certain human physical facts that should be considered any time we contemplate the computer opportunities of the future.

Most people have only five digits on each hand. A good number of people are left-handed. Vision does not usually improve with age. After hours of sitting in one place, the bones start to ache. These are just a few physical human facts. There is no reason why the physical aspects of computing should stay the same in the next century. Certainly, many facets of the desktop computer will go unchanged because of its ergonomic advantages, but in many other areas, the products won't be completely accepted until we stop trying to physically reconfigure humans.

Laptop computers have become smaller and smaller. This is what everybody wants, isn't it? Some laptop computers are so small that you can't fit your fingers on the keyboard for typing. That's a giant step backwards. If someone would invent some needle-type attachments for the fingers, then the smaller size might make sense. People's fingers are not expected to get smaller in the next 10 years, so don't build something that requires tiny fingers.

Why don't people read books on computer screens? Simple: It's not easy or comfortable. Forget about the electronic publishing of books until the aesthetic problems of reading are solved. No one wants to read a book sitting in front of a computer terminal or even on a laptop while sitting in bed. The old fashioned paper book will not be replaced until someone invents a video monitor that is easy on the eyes, fits snugly into one hand (leaving the other hand free to snack on popcorn), and can be easily read in any position in any room of the house.

Sound is a limited form of human communication. It's slow and inefficient compared to visual media (reading, pictures, graphs, etc.). Although sound will certainly play an important part in future technology—and a critical role in fields like entertainment and education—it will not become a major component of most computing fields in the next 10 years. It will remain a novelty, as has color graphics on most computers of the '80s.

My word processing software has become too complicated. I

know how to do all of the basics, like insert and delete words, but it has features that I would never dream of using. All these extra features are not bad in and of themselves, although on occasion I have unintentionally activated an unknown feature, causing panic and harm. I am not computer illiterate. I've been using, working and programming them for more than 10 years now. It's just that most software developers get carried away with features, frustrating even the most knowledgeable user. Let's keep it simple. The human mind can also be overloaded with too many features.

When designing a new future, it is important to always work within the scope of human limitation. Go Corporation's entire strategy is based on an operating system designed to serve human limitations. (Go's pen-based operating system is discussed in Chapter Five, "Hardware Triggers.") Since little in the way of human evolution is expected in the next 50 years, Go has probably made a good bet.

The following are just a few of the human limitations that should be considered in the design of future computer opportunities. Don't expect any of them to change:

- Fingers will stay the same size. Vision will not improve, nor will our hearing.

- Taste and smell are accessory senses not normally used in entertainment or education. Don't bet a bundle on them.

- Our backsides will stay in the same approximate location, allowing for age.

- Ten to 15 percent of the population will continue to be left-handed.

- The primary room for creativity will continue to be the bathroom.

- People only think about one thing at a time and it's usually the opposite sex.

There are many other human limitations to be considered when exploring future computer opportunities. Ask yourself, "Am I asking people to change or to be contortionists?" It is only a matter of looking around to find the answers. For many, these human limitàtions will be a problem. But for many more, including Go Corporation, they will be a fantastic opportunity.

Mind Levers

This chapter offers concepts to be used in conjunction with hardware triggers to generate new ideas for computer opportunities. Each concept is a mind lever designed to give a new view of solutions for old problems. When combining these abstractions with the hardware triggers in the next chapter, innovation possibilities explode.

Chapter Five
Hardware Triggers

For a new computer industry to emerge, all the required elements must come together simultaneously: The technology must be available, the price must be right and the market must demand the new product or service. A missing link will delay the growth of any computer enterprise, even those with great potential. Sometimes a technological development is the key to rapid progress. Often, a delay is caused by the high price tag of the technology. Other times the market just isn't ready for the change, though in a few years time people will embrace the new product or service anxiously.

In computer industries, the initial catalyst is technology. A new piece of equipment, when driven by the appropriate software, will trigger new computer opportunities (hence the phrase "hardware trigger"). The piece of hardware is usually not a trigger when it's first developed, because the price is initially inhibitive. The hardware becomes a trigger only when the price drops low enough to create a mass market, reducing the price further still. Occasionally, as is the case with the modem, the technology has been available for decades, and the price has been low enough to create a mass market, but the triggering effect has had to wait for corresponding markets to develop. Only in the 1990s will there be enough modems in homes to spawn many of the new on-line industries.

How Hardware Triggers Work

The desktop publishing industry is an excellent example of how a hardware trigger works. For decades typesetting was done on photo-typesetting equipment. The equipment was so expensive that only large companies and businesses that specialized in typesetting services could afford the equipment. Small publishers would send their copy out to a typesetter for conversion to high-quality print. This procedure would add one or two days to the production of any magazine or brochure. Once the typeset copy was received, it would be "pasted-up," adding artwork or photos as required by the job. This was the way the publishing industry worked, and it was the accepted method for doing business.

Even with the introduction of the computer, there was little change in the procedure. Computers were added to control the typesetting equipment, but the equipment remained horrendously expensive. It wasn't until the introduction of the low-priced laser printer that the revolution occurred. Laser printers had been around for decades, but they had always been too expensive for the average person.

The first commercially popular desktop publishing system was the Apple Macintosh with an Apple LaserWriter. The software was inadequate and the machine was underpowered, but the possibilities were immediately recognized by artists and businesses alike. The laser printer had made it possible for text and artwork to be integrated on the same printed sheet. With that, the small business was able to produce its own artwork for advertising, brochures and catalogs. Within a few years many typesetting businesses that didn't respond to the new technology closed their doors. One person with a computer, a laser printer and some sales savvy could become a low-overhead advertising agency. Desktop publishing has permanently changed the publishing, typesetting and printing businesses, and it was all triggered by a low-priced laser printer.

This part of the book will address the hardware triggers that will most likely affect the next 10 years. They are not necessarily the leading edge of technology, but they are available right now—and at a low price. This suggests that they can and are triggering new opportunities today. Newer, cutting-edge technologies are discussed later in this chapter. This newer technology is just as exciting and important as the hardware triggers of today, but generally hasn't reached the stage where an entrepreneur can put it to use, or else the price is far too high for anyone other than the largest businesses and governments to afford.

In some cases, as with the modem, the triggering equipment will act as a stopgap until newer fiber-optic and digital-cellular technology is in place. The modem will trigger new communication-linked industries in this decade, while in the next century it will likely be replaced by fiber-optic networks or other communications technology. The modem may leave us, but the industries it triggers won't. For now, the modem is one of the most important triggers of the next decade.

The hardware triggers have been divided into six groups, according to the function they perform. The first group is comprised of the communications triggers: the modem, local area network, voice mail, and fax. Next, mass storage of data with laser disk technology is reviewed. Then a close look is taken at the new approach to mobile computing with PenPad-type computers. Then come the visual triggers and audio tools that are most likely to impact us in the '90s. The last of the hardware triggers discussed is actually a collection of the other triggers that compose multimedia. Finally, we take a look at other developments in technology which, though very important, aren't likely to become commercial triggers until well into the next decade.

These sections reflect those opportunities that I feel are at hand, and, if I had the time, resources and talent, I would pursue them myself. As you read through these chapters, you may adamantly disagree with both my choices and categorizations. I may have even completely overlooked some potential triggers that you see as important elements of this decade's technology. This could well be the case. My viewpoint is from the desktop computer world out. People with a better understanding of the mainframe, minicomputer, workstation and microchip world will certainly have a different perspective. The differences and opportunities that you can see and that other people can't may be your edge. My expectation is that each person who reads this book will capture different ideas for opportunities. If this is the case, the book has served its purpose.

Communications Triggers

Centuries ago, the primary form of non-face-to-face communication was the messenger. In some cases the messenger was a pigeon (usually one-way communication), but most often it was a human. The job opportunities for a messenger were bountiful, though the pay was low and road hazards like bandits and carnivores were high.

When signal systems between mountains (smoke, mirrors, etc.) were developed, the weak messengers' union was unable to keep most of its members' jobs going. Then entered the telegraph, followed in the next century by the telephone. Communications in this century has changed forever. The telephone, found in almost every home, has transformed our society and triggered numerous commercial industries. And its work is not yet completed.

The integration of the computer with telephone systems will be a high priority for the '90s. The world is networked with telephone lines, and the possible opportunities for the computer are almost endless. The modem is more than a decade old, but indications are that the 1990s will bring it into the limelight.

Modems

There are times when I want to read the most recent news, or get the latest sports scores immediately. The newspaper is useless because its news is always at least a day old. If I catch the radio on the hour, I can hear the news, but only what the news editor feels is newsworthy. If it isn't six o'clock in the evening, network television is not available. Even on the "all-news stations," I'm at the mercy of the news editors. If I happen to find the news I want, it may not be in the detail I require.

Prodigy is an information system that subscribers can call via a modem attached to a computer. Thirteen dollars per month is the only fee required, and you can stay on the system as long as you want. Prodigy provides news, travel information, educational tasks, and consumer information, among other things. By many standards Prodigy is a fluff system. The news isn't as detailed as in the newspaper, nor as up-to-date as on radio or television. But it's there when I want it. It responds to me; I don't have to change to accommodate it. During the Soviet coup, I could get the latest headlines at my convenience. My kids use it for educational games and to cheat on computer adventure games. Last summer I used it to check out the temperature in Palm Springs before a vacation. Though Prodigy is a convenience I could easily do without, I find that my family and I are using it more and more.

Prodigy could never survive as a business on my $13 per month.

To augment its revenues the system displays advertising, and offers other services to subscribers, such as banking and travel. I'm sure the messages are financed by the advertised businesses. Prodigy is in its infancy as a business, yet this on-line system is a manifestation of the future. I expect there will be a great many more of these systems in the 1990s.

The modem is the hardware trigger for on-line information systems. These on-line information services may offer shopping by modem, news services, entertainment or education. As the number of computers attached to modems grows, the market for modem-related services will offer great opportunities. The function of a modem is to connect computers via a telephone line. The sending modem converts the computereze into signals that can be easily transmitted over an audio phone line. The receiving modem reverses the process, allowing the two computers to communicate directly.

In the mid-1980s, I set up a computer and a modem with some Bulletin Board System software to publish *ComputorEdge* Magazine (San Diego's local computer magazine, then *The Byte Buyer*), via the phone lines. People could call our computer using their modems and read the magazine without the mess of paper. That on-line publishing system continues today as a free system, and acts as *ComputorEdge*'s contribution to the San Diego computer community. The electronic magazine was designed to be a test of a much bigger future market where the primary source of information would be the computer. The design was for the system to be supported primarily by advertising.

At that time, there were numerous on-line information services that could be accessed by modem, but they all charged by the hour. Calling Dialog or CompuServe was similar to making a long distance phone call: The longer you stayed on the line, the more you paid. This was fine for the researcher or stock analyst, but for casual browsers of information, the cost was prohibitive. I believed then, as I believe now, that the future of on-line information systems was in free, or practically free systems supported by advertising. *The Byte Buyer On-Line* was designed to be such a system, yet today it continues to be a cost, generating no income. What went wrong?

In order to sell advertising, a newspaper must have readers, a radio station must have listeners, a television network must have viewers.

It is a pure numbers problem. If a medium has high enough numbers, advertising can be sold. For an electronic on-line information source to sell advertising, it must have regular subscribers or readers—a great quantity of readers. How much the business can charge for advertising depends on how many qualified people the advertising will reach. This presents the unique problem of computer on-line systems.

In the mid-1980s, 1200-baud modems were considered state-of-the-art for affordable modems. 1200 baud represented a transmission rate of approximately 200 words per minute. This was considerably better than the older 300 baud, but for people receiving information over the phone line it was still too time consuming. To transfer the entire magazine to a reader would have taken 80 minutes. If the average reader were to stay on-line for 30 minutes, that would allow only 48 readers a day. If we added 10 phone lines, we could accommodate 480 readers a day. For the cost of operations, that would not be enough readers to charge the advertising rates needed for a profitable business.

Over the next few years, 2400-baud modems took over as the standard low-cost modem, but this only doubled the speed and, therefore, the potential readers. In the 1990s, the 9600 baud modem will become the standard, greatly enhancing the on-line market. But modem speed had not been the only problem with my system.

Modem sales have traditionally lagged behind the sales of computers. Most people who would buy a computer found little or no need to buy a modem. That meant that even if you considered everyone who owned a computer in 1985, most of them would never have been able to use your system because they didn't have a modem. The market for free on-line systems just wasn't large enough at that time. In the 1990s this is changing, and rapidly. In the early '90s, the sales of modems are outstripping computer sales by a factor of three to one. Many computer users are now checking out what's available on the phone lines. My company's book *How to Get Started with Modems* has moved from an OK seller to a best seller. If the free on-line market does not develop in the 1990s, it won't be for lack of a market.

The modem itself is probably a temporary, interim instrument of communication. It has been with us for decades, yet its limitations doom its continued use in the early decades of the next century. As we become cabled together with fiber optics, the higher transmission speeds of direct connection will displace this stopgap device. Even though the modem may go to the wayside, the industries it will trigger in the 1990s will stay with us, growing stronger than ever.

Modems and the Media

When computers become the dominant source for news and entertainment, programming will become timeless. There will be no schedule for when the news will be presented: It will always be available and continuously updated. The computer will be the news-wire to which everyone has access. The readers or viewers will be able to go directly to the news of most interest to them, either scanning or continuing to dig deeper.

Modems and Education

Homework will be delivered via modem from the school directly into the home. The student will use the computer and modem to do research via the school library's computer system.

Modems and Travel

Travel agencies will transform into computer systems driven by information. Customers will make their reservations directly with airlines and hotels. Special systems will help them plan their vacations, giving recommendations. Would-be vacationers will explore travel possibilities in the convenience of their own homes.

Modems and Shopping

Shopping by modem will have several advantages over today's shopping. First, you'll never have to leave your home. If a company has its catalog on-line, a simple phone call will allow you to place your order. Second, shopping by modem will cut out the middleman. This usually adds up to savings. Modem shopping services will proliferate in the '90s; consumers will find more opportunities to buy directly from an airline, manufacturer or publisher. Some of the features that Prodigy already offers are shopping and banking by modem.

These ideas are all industries that could be triggered by the modem today. Some of these systems exist today, but are so new they haven't gained popular acceptance. As more computers and modems enter homes, these ideas may prove to be very lucrative enterprises. Some people project that by the end of this century, a modem will be standard equipment on every computer.

Local Area Networks

My first experience with a desktop computer was a personal revelation. It was not a powerful computer by today's standards, but the possibilities overwhelmed me. I could write letters without worrying about typos. I could organize databases for my personal use. Most of all, the computer represented my opportunities for the future. The projects I built on my computer in early 1981 barely scratched the surface of the meager computing power of my machine, yet I sat in awe of its capabilities.

It was a powerful feeling.

I did not experience that feeling of unexplored power again until 1990, when I started using our newly installed Local Area Network. Prior to 1990 the business had grown rapidly, including the addition of several new computers. We kept our business organized by delegating specific tasks to specific machines.

On the occasions when we needed to share data, we would copy the pertinent data onto a floppy diskette and walk it to the appropriate machine. (This is known as SneakerNet.) While inconvenient, it was effective and helped to keep things organized. Because only one person could use a particular computer at a time, we operated from printed reports of data.

I knew that eventually we would need a local area network that would tie all our computers together.

My resistance to networks was not unlike the resistance of the new computer buyer. "It looks too complicated and costs too much." "I don't know how to work the thing." "I don't really need it to do my business." In spite of all my stalling, I knew that to progress I needed to connect my sales department computers to the same database. I took the plunge.

Within two weeks of network installation, all my salespeople were working from the same database. I was able to review and analyze the status of the business without leaving my office.

One day while I was perusing the company databases, I was overcome by the same feeling that had captured me nine years before. The synergy of all the computers working in parallel was creating a greater whole than I could comprehend. We had done more than merely tie a number of computers together—we had created a collaboration of minds.

One computer with one user is limited by both the machine and the operator. It is a world unto itself, locked into an internalization process with little access to the outside. The wonder of the modem is its ability to open up the outside world to the computer owner. The network creates the same outside connections, only multiplied by the number of computer users.

The local area network will be one of the greatest hardware triggers of the next 10 years because it is a powerful tool of collaboration, and because it is here today, ready to use.

How Does It Work?

There are three primary functions of a network: moving data between computers, sharing data simultaneously between two or more users, and sharing peripheral devices like printers and scanners. All the computers are connected via a series of wires, with the appropriate hardware and software to manage the communications. In the most powerful networks, one computer is usually dedicated to act as a "network server." The server handles all the communications, data storing and sharing functions, and peripheral assignment. The server has no user, but responds to requests from other computer users on the system.

In today's business system, the LAN is used to store all the company-wide data and the programs that use that data. To a computer user on the network, the server looks like part of the computer user's system, and is just as easy to use. All the salespeople can simultaneously share and update the same customer list. Sales orders can be placed while the accounting department has real-time access to the same information.

Most of today's LAN applications are in the business world, but when looked upon as a tool of collaboration, numerous relatively unexplored opportunities in other professions present themselves.

Entertainment

The entertainment industry has beaten us to death with one-on-one entertainment. The television is a monogamous relationship between the viewer and the box. We become entranced with the programming, not even allowing a break for commercial messages. Films and videos are of the same nature, though in a theater you can ignore hundreds of other people at the same time. Our entertainment has become an exercise in isolation. The time has come for collaborative entertainment.

*   *   *

To play football, it takes a team of players. To run a starship, it requires an entire crew. As you enter the 21st Century Gaming Room with 12 of your best buddies, you know that you've been well prepared for your mission of exploring the universe, battling any dangers you may encounter.

You and your friends have drawn lots to see who will be the Captain, the First Officer, Weapons Control, Navigation, Helmsman, etc. You'll each have a separate battle station that will be a computer tied to the network. You may battle against the computer or other teams of adventurers like yourselves.

Your Saturday entertainment is now a collaboration of minds in a team effort to overcome adversity. The stage is set and the scenarios are controlled by the server.

*   *   *

The network is a tool for creating unsurpassed entertainment. The technology to create it is here today.

Education

Much like the entertainment industry, education is a relationship between the student and the instructor. Yes, there are other students in the class, but in most cases student-to-student relationships are social. The power of the network can bring collaboration to the learning environment that will not only stimulate, but also greatly increase the productivity of our best teachers.

* * *

All the students have computers at their desks that are hooked into the server computer. Freddy is King Louis the Sixteenth. He is interacting with his advisors, who are students receiving the same information on their computers that the real Louis' advisors had available. The people are in a violent mood and Freddy must make the best decision to save his neck, the crown and France. After an intense series of political moves, Freddy eventually abdicates, saving his neck and France while losing his crown.

In a review of the actual French Revolution, the students question why the real Louis refused to see the light and literally lost his head. The smugness of power, the changing philosophy of the times and the underpinnings of change are hot topics for discussion. By the end of the session the students feel as if they lived through the French Revolution.

* * *

Simulation technology has been used for decades in the military for collaborative training, which emulates battle conditions in the classroom. Today the technology is available—and inexpensive enough to apply to our schools. This and many other educational uses of networks will come about in the next 10 years. The only question is, who will be the people to do it?

What are the opportunities for networks in medicine, crime prevention or domestic engineering? Are home security and family life issues candidates for the collaborative technology of networks?

Voice Mail

Almost every home has at least one telephone. It is our primary connection with the outside world. If our phone goes dead, we feel helpless and isolated. Few people know anyone who is telephone illiterate. It is the easiest electronic device to use. For these reasons, voice mail applications will explode in the 1990s.

Voice mail hardware is a sound card that installs into a computer. It is capable of both sending and receiving digitized sound. Digitized sound is audio that has been converted to bits for storage on computer media, like hard disk drives. The voice card will serve the same function as a telephone answering machine with a couple of major advantages.

In voice mail, the response to a call can be tailored according to the actions of the caller on the telephone. "Push 'one' to receive a recorded message about our services." "Push 'two' to talk to a salesperson." "Push 'three' to leave a message." These prerecorded computer messages are automatically sent to the caller. When the caller responds, the computer moves to another part of the program and continues with new messages.

In some cities, voice mail systems have been set up for electronic dating services. The computer handles all the work, while the only interaction is between the callers. Many banks in the United States use voice mail for customers making account inquiries. Voice mail technology can easily be used for crude expert systems that will supply problem-solving information to callers.

Here is an example of a possible commercial use for voice mail:

*   *   *

The computer system stores a database of restaurant information in a local area. A young couple is trying to decide where to go for dinner. They call Restaurant Tonight, the voice mail restaurant service. When the computer answers the phone, it sends a message for the caller to select "one" to hear about restaurants by food type and "two" for restaurants by area. The next message gives a listing of types or areas depending on the caller's selection. The caller makes another selection. The names of the restaurants are listed. If the caller selects a certain restaurant, a message will give information about that location, and possibly even what the specials are for that evening.

*   *   *

This restaurant voice mail system could be financed either by a per-call charge or, more likely, by charging local restaurants for their participation in the system. This service could be applied to almost any occupation. All that's required is a need for available information.

To set up a voice mail system, a voice mail card is installed in a computer. The card connects directly to the telephone system with features for answering the line. Large-capacity mass-storage devices are required, since digitized audio consumes a great deal of space. The amount of storage required depends on the amount of information on the system. If an expert information system is being installed, the huge capacity of a gigabyte hard drive or a rewritable laser disk storage device may be required.

Fax

Facsimile technology has been with us for decades, but in the late '80s it became the messenger of choice for many business. The price is low, and with computers, the '90s will bring many more fax machines into both businesses and homes. Today it's less expensive to send a fax many places in the world than it is to mail a letter. Watch out postal services!

A fax machine may be a separate device, or a special board installed in a computer. There are advantages and disadvantages to both. Fax machines move paper copies across the telephone lines: paper in one end, a copy out the other. Though reception of a fax may be slow on a computer, computer-generated faxes can be customized and sent to many different parties automatically.

The fax machine alone has been a tremendous growth industry, but when coupled with the power of the computer the opportunities abound.

For example, Corky Deeds of Lightspeed in San Diego has put together a system he calls "AutoFAX." Using a computer with both voice mail and fax boards, his system will provide interactive information to anyone with a telephone and a fax machine. When a person calls AutoFAX via the telephone, the computer responds with a voice-mail message. The caller enters in the number of the desired information, and his or her fax number, on the telephone touchtone pad. After completing the call, the requested information is automatically transmitted to the caller's fax machine. No computer or modem is required by the user—just a telephone and a fax machine.

This AutoFAX system could be used to set up our voice-mail restaurant information system, only now the entire menu could be faxed to our caller. Any time people want information of a specific nature, an AutoFAX computer system could be set up to supply it. The uses range from computer dating services to political lobbying.

Information Storage Triggers

As a business grows, the number of filing cabinets grows proportionately. There is always more paper, either new or historical, that needs a home. This is one of the problems of an information age: We never have enough closet space. With computers we need electronic closet space. The electronic closet of the '80s, and the primary storage device in a computer system, was the hard disk drive. The hard disk drive is a recording device that's been pounded into the shape of a disk, placed in a hermetically sealed box and attached to a computer to save bytes of data. In the early '80s, a hard disk drive for a desktop computer was relatively expensive. My first drive was 10 megabytes (approximately 10 million bytes of computer storage capacity), and cost about $1,000. At this writing, I can buy a 200 megabyte drive (20 times the capacity of my first drive) for about $600, and the unit is much smaller and faster.

In almost every new computer industry, the hard disk drive has been an integral hardware trigger. The hard disk drive will continue to be integral to all new computer industries, but it is not discussed at great length in this book for the same reason the desktop computer is only touched upon lightly: The hard disk drive is so important to computer systems that it has become part of every useful system. Whether you're working with a multimedia system, using a network or buying a computer for your kids, you should have a hard disk drive. I expect that even on PenPad-type computers there will be a demand for a mass storage device, probably a hard disk drive.

Today hard disk drives are available with gigabyte capacity (more than 1,000 times my original hard drive) and faster access speeds than ever. Currently there is no end in sight for magnetic hard disk drive technology. Though the hard disk drive will continue to dominate, there is a newcomer that will be supplementing the hard drive, improving the physical portability of data and adding more storage to our computer system: optical laser disk drives.

Optical Laser Disk Drives

The term "laser disk" applies to a family of devices that, via optical laser technology, store computer information and data. Most of the '80s were spent developing laser disk technology, and in 1990 it was just beginning to come into its own. What is the significance of laser disk technology? How will it trigger new opportunities in the future? To answer these questions we will review the recent history of computer information storage.

In the beginning (the 1960s and 1970s), magnetic media was used to store computer data, usually recording tape or diskettes. The recording tape could hold huge amounts of data, but it was comparatively slow since you had to wind through the tape to find various pieces of data. The disk medium was developed to overcome the winding and rewinding problems, since the reading device could

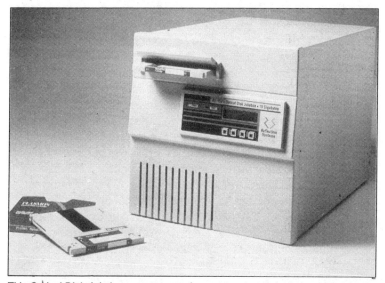

This Optical Disk Jukebox can store and access up to 11 gigabytes of data, yet is small enough to fit on a desktop.

move directly to the desired location on the diskette, hence saving time. But since the diskettes were flat and round rather than continuous, they were physically limited in the amount of data they could store. It remained to be seen how you could get both speed and adequate storage capacity in magnetic disk technology.

Through the '80s, manufacturers continued to increase the speed and capacity of magnetic disk drives to the point where the individual computer user could purchase 30 or more times what was available in the early eighties. The price was the same, or lower, and the package was physically smaller. Even with these gains, this form of storage technology was not keeping pace with the demands of computer applications available. Computer Aided Design (CAD), graphics, DeskTop Publishing (DTP), voice digitizing and many more computer uses were demanding more storage space. At this writing, gigabyte (1,024,000,000 characters of data) and higher magnetic hard disk drives are available in the standard 5¼-inch size.

The larger-capacity drives created a new problem: How do we transport those huge volumes of data? It was recognized early on that laser disk technology had the potential to open entirely new worlds of computing. Where magnetic disk drives could store huge data blocks, laser disk technology could potentially store one to two gigabytes of data on removable hard optical diskettes. (In 1991, CD-ROM [Compact Disc–Read-Only Memory] drives typically could store 650 megabytes of data, depending on the size of the optical diskette.) This greater amount of storage enhanced space-consuming applications like digitized video and sound, as well as making it possible to include entire libraries—even a set of encyclopedias—on one diskette. But most importantly, the disk can be easily changed. In just a few seconds, the computer user can change the diskette to access another vast library of programs or data. Worlds of information become available on a single, removable optical diskette.

Today CD-ROM titles that can be accessed by most types of computers include: multimedia encyclopedias with multiple search paths, multimedia games that talk, business directories, medical information, voter registration lists, meteorological data, video, photography and art clips, world atlases that zoom from the globe to cities, language dictionaries and courses, interactive educational titles with sound and video, and much more. This is a market that's only in its infancy. It doesn't take much imagination to see the possibilities.

In the '80s, the major disadvantage to laser disk technology was that the data could not be erased and rewritten. (CD-ROM titles cannot be altered.) Once the diskette recorded data, the change to the diskette was physical and permanent. It could not be cleared for reuse. This severely limited the potential of laser technology until the early 1990s, when the first erasable optical mass storage devices became available. With the introduction of erasable optical disks, many new editing and sorting functions—previously the exclusive realm of the hard disk drive—can be performed with laser technology.

The CD-ROM has another problem: slow access time. Most CD-ROMs require that data be read into memory before being displayed. Between that step, the slowness of the drives, and the vast amounts of data to be moved, the process can seem painfully slow for many multimedia applications. This problem will go away sometime during this decade with faster computers and optical drives. Even with all its present deficiencies, laser disk technology remains a power stimulus for many new opportunities.

Optical mass storage technology is the trigger required for many computer industries of the future. Applications that make extensive use of video, animation and sound will see an immediate benefit, but many of the following applications are also growing out of this technology.

Expert Systems

To be an expert, you must digest and analyze volumes of data. To our credit, humans have not run into the limits of the storage space in their heads. Though many may fail to use the space, there is no known case of someone running out of room in their brain. (The "Brain is Full" message would appear.)

The object of an expert computer system would be to combine the knowledge of one or more human experts into a single computer system organized for research, analysis and/or problem solving. Theoretically, an expert system would proceed through the same steps as a human expert, asking questions and responding with the appropriate information. It's even likely that the expert computer system would actually be more thorough and accurate than the human expert. The computer does not forget. Of course, this accuracy would depend upon the validity of the data and the programming of the system. (Even expert systems only do what they're told to do by the program, though the system's analysis may return results that no one expected.)

In medicine, an expert system could be used to help guide doctors through an especially difficult diagnosis. The system would be built by doctors and used by doctors. Teachers could build expert systems for education. Police departments could build expert systems for law enforcement. The primary dilemma is having enough storage capacity to save and manipulate the information. This problem can be solved by laser disk technology.

Crude forms of these expert systems exist today as databases that can be purchased on CD-ROM. These will continue to proliferate and become more sophisticated. Anyone who has a reason to collect and review data will be in a position to pursue one of these opportunities.

Scientific Research

In many areas of science there is more data than information. The abundance of data is so overwhelming to the human mind that there is little or no comprehension. With large storage devices, the data can be organized and manipulated until patterns appear. Chaos becomes information. The capacities of laser disk technology are a boon to scientific research.

Data sharing will become easier when gigabytes of data can be loaded onto an optical diskette and mailed to another scientific unit. In the 1990s, optical disk drives will become standard on workstations for engineering and scientific applications. They won't replace hard disk drives, but will become a system complement.

Multimedia

I have devoted a later section of this chapter to multimedia because it is the best bet for bringing the computer into homes around the world. Commodore's CDTV is already sneaking computers into the homes of people who think they're just buying a CD player.

Multimedia makes computers the television sets of the future.

Now, with laser disk technology in place, the multimedia revolution of the '90s is about to take off. Starting with the CD-ROM, laser disk technology will be required for video images, animated sequences and digitized audio, the basics of multimedia.

Verbum Magazine is available on the Macintosh as an interactive magazine. Using art, music, video clips, voice and print, this CD-ROM magazine interacts with the reader on all these levels simultaneously. One portion of the magazine displays art or photographs of free-lance contributors, with explanations in the voice of the artist or photographer. Another section offers a panel discussion of computer experts answering the key issues of multimedia technology. As the reader selects an expert to answer a question, a video clip supplies the answer in the voice and image of the panelist. This collaboration of experts was actually created through separate interviews combined later on the computer. San Diego-based *Verbum* is working on other formats for their interactive magazine.

The technology is here, the price is down and the market is growing. Laser disk technology is positioned well to trigger many of the new computer industries that will require massive volumes of data, whether information, video or audio, at a user's fingertips. The possibilities given here are only a few of the many opportunities that will be derived from laser disk technology.

Mobile Hardware Triggers

Laptop, palmtop and other forms of mobile computers found in the early 1990s are stopgap machines for portable computing, just as the modem is stopgap technology for computer communications. The work currently being done with new types of operating systems and computer hardware is too innovative to bode well for the interim machine called a laptop computer.

PenPad-Type Computers

Rex, a claims adjuster for an automobile insurance company, is on his way to view the remains of another automobile. Upon arriving at the site of the wreck, he hops out of his car with his notebook computer in hand. This type of notebook computer has become commonplace by the year 2000, and looks nothing like what was called a notebook computer in the year 1990.

In 1990, the notebook computer was an ultra-light computer with all the features of a desktop computer, including an almost-complete keyboard. Of course, the keys were so small that typing was tedious and difficult. In those days, the notebook computer was used primarily by traveling executives and salespeople. There was usually a supplemental desktop computer at the office or at home.

In the year 2000 we still see models of computers similar to the 1990 notebook, but their primary use is for keyboard data input. And even that isn't necessary since anyone can now purchase a keyboard to plug into their PenPad-type notebook computer. The PenPad computer has become the instrument of choice for many professions that require field work. The sales volume of these machines has grown to match that of traditional desktop computers. PenPad computers are not a replacement for the versatile desktop computers, but rather an able partner, creating new computer industries. The Pen-Pad revolution of the '90s has been likened to the microcomputer revolution of the '80s, changing society in ways that were only science fiction a decade before.

In September 1987, GO Corporation was established. Founded by a group of computer professionals, GO was dedicated to developing a new way to compute. It didn't intend to replace the desktop computer, but to supplement the technology with tools for the mobile professional. Its mission was to develop a pen-based computer operating system that made it possible for people to work in the most familiar way: with a pen.

Rather than attach new equipment to old computer notions, the GO design team tossed out the old computer concepts. Working to learn from the industry's past mistakes, they designed their entire operating system with the future in mind.

The computer became a pad. The input device became a pen. Movements and gestures of the pen became commands. Changing programs was as easy as flipping the page of a book with a finger. The PenPad computers would be light, mobile and as easy to use as a clipboard. When the founders of GO stated that they were developing this new operating system for salespeople, service technicians, managers, field engineers, insurance agents and adjustors, and government inspectors, they knew in their hearts that these first applications would only be scratching the surface of the potential of PenPad computing. But even they didn't predict that by the year 2000 a startling 50 percent of computer sales would be PenPad-type computers, most using GO's PenPoint™ operating system.

Beginning in 1992, the PenPad-type computer rapidly became an integral part of the predicted occupations, like insurance claims adjusting. Almost all the major computer manufacturers jumped in quickly to build their own PenPad machines. This new way of computing, almost unknown in the late 1980s, became the hottest portion of the PC market.

Strangely enough, the winners in the PenPad computer race were not the expected IBM or Apple, but rather some upstart unknowns who had mortgaged their homes in the early 1990s to finance their manufacturing ventures.

In the year 2000, you are as likely to see a PenPad computer as you are a briefcase. They are being used in all the schools. Each student has a desk computer that is connected to the classroom network. (Micro-cellular connections have replaced the old modem and wire connections.) Homework is uploaded to the PenPad, and the computer is toted home. The excuse for incomplete homework has become, ". . . the dog ate my computer."

Doctors and hospitals are using PenPad computers for medical records. The computers are hooked into an expert medical system; while the doctor notes the patient's responses to symptomatic questions, the answers are recorded with the stroke of a pen. Treatment and pharmaceutical prescriptions can be ordered directly through the PenPad system.

PenPad computers have become the essential tool of crime investigation. When returning from the scene of a crime, the evidence that has been entered and classified at the scene can be downloaded for immediate analysis by the main computers. The quicker response by the computer systems caused a dramatic increase in fast solutions to criminal investigations.

For graphic artists, the PenPad has replaced the desktop computer and mouse. The desktop computer had always been a tedious disappointment to many artists; PenPad computers were finally a medium that was a natural complement to the talent of the hand.

Industry uses desk-sized and wall-sized PenPad monitors to review their designs and work directly on their project plans. Computer Aided Design (CAD) has been almost completely transferred to PenPad computers—they are easier, quicker and more natural to use than the old computer tablets.

By the year 2000, there is almost no industry that hasn't been transformed in some way by the work of the founders of GO and the PenPoint™ operating system.

*   *   *

The preceding section is a combination of fact and speculation. PenPoint™ exists, and pen-based computer systems are available, but the applications are just beginning to scratch the surface.

As of the end of 1991, many PenPad-type computers have been introduced. For a number of years, Grid Systems has had an operational machine based on the MS-DOS operating system. (Grid has announced that it also plans to support the PenPoint™ operating system.) Microsoft has introduced *Windows* for Pen Computing, which runs under MS-DOS. Momenta has introduced an MS-DOS-based PenPad-type computer. Most of the major computer manufacturers (IBM, NCR, etc.) have announced their intention to support Go's PenPoint™ operating system. There is a great deal of interest and activity in this market, and products are at hand.

How It Works

There are two key components to a PenPad-type computer. The first is the tablet—in actuality, the computer. The tablet looks like a flat board with a video screen. It can come in almost any size, from small enough to be hidden in the palm of your hand to large enough to cover a wall.

The second component is the pen, or stylus. The stylus is a pen-shaped object used on the tablet much as a pen is used on paper. The computer responds to the movement of the stylus. The computer can learn to read handwriting or respond to gestures. Gestures are natural movements often made by people using a pen and paper. For

Momenta's "Pentop" computer uses an electronic stylus that writes directly on a flat-panel screen.

example, a line through a word would mean to delete that word. If the computer senses the gesture of the stylus putting a line through a word, it will respond by allowing that deletion to occur. An up arrow could mean the desire to insert a word.

Under the PenPoint™ operating system, computer information is organized similar to a notebook, with tabs along the edge for each section of the notebook. To turn the tab you merely do the page-turning gesture on the tab, and the computer moves you to the appropriate location. These features are built into the operating system; therefore, all applications will operate in a similar manner.

The Potential

Software applications and vertical markets are virtually unlimited when you allow your mind to wander. For example, the size of a PenPoint™ screen may be as small as your watch face, or as large as your conference room wall. The operating system is designed to take advantage of the best features of both. What could you do with a

PenPad computer that had a screen as large as your wall? Group brainstorming, engineering design work, interactive entertainment — it boggles the mind.

Historically, a new type of computer and a new way of doing things has spawned numerous entrepreneurial opportunities. When IBM introduced the IBM PC, the desktop computer market and thousands of new hardware and software companies took off with the idea. The Apple Macintosh had a similar impact in graphics

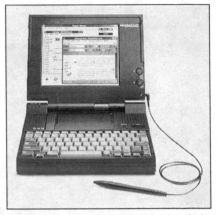

The TouchPen is a high-resolution handwriting digitizer designed for portable PCs running Microsoft *Windows* for Pen Computing, Go PenPoint™ or MS-DOS applications.

and art applications, though to a lesser extent. PenPad computing has enough advantages—and is enough of a change from standard desktop computing—that its reverberations could easily be as heavy as that of the IBM PC.

Visual Hardware Triggers

Our eyes are a primary receiver of communications. In today's society we use eyes to receive information more than any other sense. We can read much faster than an instructor can speak. A picture is worth a thousand words. Without a visual medium, the computer, regardless of its power, becomes slow and awkward. The video displays and printers have been a significant source of hardware triggers in the 1980s, and will continue to be an integral part of many new industries.

During the '80s there were three primary visual technologies that changed the way we work. The first was the improvement in the digital color video display. The fuzzy picture of the early '80s has been continually upgraded with higher resolutions and more available colors. The improvements have made the computer a tool of artists and dreamers as well as business people. The possibility of the computer replacing the television is real, though a smart compromise is more likely. In any case, the television and the computer video monitor will continue as two distinct entities in households through this decade, with applications like multimedia bridging the gap between the two.

High-Resolution Color Graphics

With a few graphic exceptions, the improved quality of color graphics has had minimal impact on the general business community to date. Since the improvement of video graphics technology on desktop computers, graphic-oriented fields like engineering use PCs for schematic diagrams and engineering drawings. Yet most businesses and individuals are buying the latest video displays merely because they prefer to have the best, not because they want a functional value added to their system.

Improved graphics has actually added very little value to most business computing applications. The majority of users are still doing word processing, spreadsheets and database management. Very few spend much time building pretty charts.

The greatest benefit from new video technology has been in the graphic arts and desktop publishing fields. High-quality color on PCs has revolutionized the way these fields function. Yet graphics work remains only a small part of the business.

In the future, however, new multimedia, entertainment and educational applications will change high-resolution color from a "nice to have" into a "must have."

Laser Printers

Another major visual device of the '80s was the laser printer. After making a spectacular entrance, it has rapidly become the standard printer for any new computer system. As the price drops, it will replace the dot-matrix printer as the leading seller in printers. By the end of the decade, the dot-matrix printer will be a specialized machine reserved for applications peculiar to its strengths.

Color Printers

A truly fascinating development coming into its own in the '90s is the color printer. As artists developed their work on multicolored computers in the '80s, they were frustrated by the difficulty of reproducing their work anywhere but on their color computer monitor. The most common method of reproduction was a color slide taken directly from the screen. In the late '80s and early '90s, color printers rapidly entered the market.

Initially, the price of high-quality printers made them accessible only to certain businesses that could sell their work as a service. In the early '90s the price of color printers began to fall rapidly. It is expected that by the middle of the decade the price may be low enough to spark more new business opportunities.

*   *   *

Instant color greeting cards tailored to each buyer could be printed on the spot. Different artwork or even home video scenes could be included in each card. Today's cost for printing from an available color printer would be less than 50 cents each, depending on the printer's quality. (This cost will drop with each passing year.) Selling at $2.00 each, a profit could be made. Have you checked the price of greeting cards lately? What about children's books, or T-shirts?

*   *   *

The Scanner As a Trigger

In the mid-'80s, the scanner entered the desktop computer market in conjunction with desktop publishing. The scanner is a device that reads a document or graphic into a digital form that can be stored and used by a computer. For example, a photograph can be scanned into a computer file, then displayed on the screen. On-screen the computer can modify the photo: enlarge it, scale it down, mix it with text, or modify it in a number of other ways. The new work can then be printed to a laser printer or a higher-quality imagesetter.

With special optical-character-reading software, scanners can convert documents to word processing files, often saving hours or weeks of data input. In publishing, special color scanners are being used to create the color separations used in large printing operations. Scanner technology is a way for us to convert our visual images to computer-useable data.

Optical scanners are used by companies that specialize in converting books and long documents to computer format, and also by those that specialize in restoring old photographs. Recent developments with color scanners have brought their prices down to the point where it's almost as cheap to buy color as black and white (greyscale). As scanner technology improves in the '90s, many more opportunities will be triggered for anyone who has a need to convert visual information to computer format, and back to visual information.

When a new computer industry is triggered by these types of visual hardware, it will usually be in collaboration with other types of hardware, for example, laser disk drives—removable media with high storage capacity. Higher-quality output will require larger amounts of mass storage. Improvement in one technology alone will not do the job. In new applications like multimedia, exceptional visual output will be expected.

Audio Hardware Triggers

The computer has made great strides in the last decade as a transmitter of sounds. It reproduces everything from full musical scores to the human voice. Some of the most powerful hardware triggers for the next decade will use computers as sound transmitters and receivers.

The problems of some audio reception applications, like voice recognition, are much more complicated than the simple reproduction of sound. To understand the language of a human voice, the computer must be able to differentiate dialects, varying voice tones and context changes. This is a tedious process for a machine that can only do one small thing at a time.

The human brain literally processes millions of bits of data simultaneously for both sight and voice recognition. While computers have made some progress, they lag behind even the slowest of humans by a huge margin in this category, only understanding very limited vocabularies.

Sound Cards

Sound cards will become standard on computers in the next decade for the same reason that people buy high-quality graphics: The games will be more exciting. (On computers like the Amiga, Tandy and Macintosh, sound is already standard equipment.) Most computer game producers are now adding music to their adventures. To take full advantage of the games' features, enhanced sound capabilities are required.

Sound cards have already triggered the computer music industry. Along with the MIDI musical interface, which attaches piano-like keyboards and other instruments to computers, enhanced sound capabilities have triggered many changes in the music industry. It has become common for musicians, both amateur and professional, to use computers to write, arrange and produce music.

Most computers can be used to write and arrange music as long as they have a music capability and the proper software. If the computer does not come with sound capability, an add-on board can be purchased as an upgrade. Computer music has already become a major business in the United States. One of the new growth areas for computer-produced and reproduced digitized music in the '90s is expected to be multimedia applications. The MIDI musical interface has become a standard for computer-generated music, and it is expected that this market will continue to grow.

The multimedia applications currently being produced on the CD-ROM format require enhanced sound. The articles in CD-ROM encyclopedias can talk you through a video animation. Or, a book of quotations will give you John F. Kennedy's digitized voice with his most famous speeches.

Voice Control

The technology is here for limited-vocabulary voice control, but the applications are currently confined to specialized markets. Until the general market sees a need to add voice control to its systems, this type of hardware is unlikely to trigger any growth industries.

Voice control and recognition are used extensively on computer projects for the disabled, and could be used in educational applications such as teaching children to read or teaching a foreign language.

But using voice control as an integral part of these applications will require more advances in the technology.

Configurations of visual and audio hardware triggers are being used to enhance both the entertainment and education industries. Each new combination makes other ideas possible. In the next section, visual and audio triggers are combined with laser disk and video technology to create new multimedia industries like Desktop Video (DTV). Multimedia is an excellent example of how hardware triggers will blend in new combinations to create new opportunities.

Multimedia Hardware Triggers

I have included this particular section not because multimedia is responsible for the spawning of one or two hardware triggers, but because it is the product of numerous computer hardware triggers. Multimedia will determine the future of the television set. It is certainly one of the most dramatic demonstrations of computer power. No one can walk away from a multimedia demonstration without being impressed. Nor can anyone walk away without wanting a multimedia computer system. For years the price has been too high for the average person, but in the '90s these prices are plummeting.

What Is Multimedia?

Multimedia is the combining of audio and video with the power of computers to produce entertainment, educational tools and other applications that use music, voice, sound effects, video animation and/or graphics. Ultimately, the components of a multimedia system could include your television, video camera, videotape recorder, audio equipment, CD player and many more pieces of equipment. The computer brings them all together.

This trademarked symbol denotes a PC system with multimedia capabilities.

Multimedia is not a job for the average computer. With the exception of Commodore's Amiga, most computers require the top-of-the-line model with extensive upgrades to become adequate multimedia machines. The multimedia extension for Microsoft *Windows* requires high-quality sound and video upgrades, a CD-ROM drive, hard disk drive and a fast computer with a minimum of two megabytes of memory. The primary addition to the most powerful Macintosh is a CD-ROM drive. Most multimedia applications are heavily dependent on CD-ROM technology.

In the '80s we became accustomed to the Video Cassette Recorder (VCR). Sales of VCRs exploded, with the machines entering millions

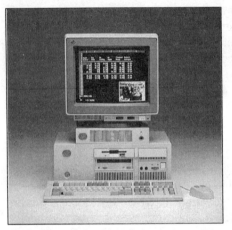

of homes. Parallel to the VCR was the Compact Disc (CD) player. The CD player has become the replacement for the ancient record player. Records have only retained their value as collector's items. In the course of this invasion of consumer electronics, we have become acclimated to the look and feel of the electronic entertainment box. Now, there is a new box with the same look and feel as the CD player or VCR: the

IBM's "Ultimedia" multimedia computer system

Commodore CDTV (Commodore Dynamic Total Vision). CDTV looks like a CD-ROM player or VCR, and may be the next step in home entertainment. But this entertainment box is not as innocuous as it looks.

Many people over the years have vowed to never allow a computer into their home. An occasional video game machine is all right, but not a full-blown computer. This is the secret of CDTV: It's a complete and powerful Amiga computer in disguise. It has all the features of a computer, but looks like a VCR. Anything you can do

Building fantasy worlds with Virtual Reality.

with most computers you can do with CDTV—and in many cases, you can do them better. If the general public doesn't catch on, many households could unknowingly become computerized. The price is also deceptively low. If Commodore pulls this off, the computer opportunities generated by this cloaked device will be incredible. CDTV is definitely an interactive, multimedia device. Similar in concept to CDTV is CD-I (Compact Disc–Interactive). CD-I is the primary competing technology for CDTV.

Virtual Reality

Multimedia is the integration of sight, sound and computer. Its interactive applications can give you the visual quality of television, the audio attributes of a stereo and the interaction of a computer. Potential uses of multimedia could capture you in an entrancing environment, such as visiting the ruins of ancient Greece, taking a stroll through the design of a yet-to-be-built house, or fighting a battle in a vivid adventure game.

The popular term is "virtual reality." We are able to travel to remote locations without moving from our seat. In some cases, devices like stereoscopic helmets and instrumented gloves provide three-dimensional scenery and interactive responses to our movements. The more sophisticated applications with special helmets and gloves may not have much impact in the '90s, but virtual reality will undoubtedly have tremendous impact in both entertainment and education. An interactive device providing animation, speech, music and response is an irresistible platform.

Multimedia applications don't have to be exotic adventures. For example, in the process of doing research for this book, I put together a multimedia computer system. Then, using a digital camera built by Logitech and a Sony microphone, I was able to produce a multimedia scrapbook of my family. The opening scene on the computer shows a collage of our pictures. As the reader selects various buttons on the screen, new pictures are brought into view. In the background, you hear different family members explaining the scenes in their own digitized voices. With my digital camera and microphone, I could produce multimedia scrapbooks for anyone who would like some electronic memories.

Although it is possible to perform multimedia applications on

The Mandala Virtual Reality System allows you to create interactive environments that can be entered and controlled through the use of any video camera.

most computer systems, the Commodore Amiga and Apple Macintosh computers have taken an early lead in applications. What has made the Amiga the choice of many professionals is its multiple processor design. Unlike the Mac and IBM-compatible machines, which force the majority of the work through one main microprocessor, the Amiga computer divides the tasks between multiple processors. With the Video Toaster upgrade (discussed later), functions like three-dimensional animation (difficult at best on Macs, and almost impossible without major upgrades on IBM compatibles) are relatively easy on the Amiga. What may give Amiga an even greater advantage is its reputation for low cost, especially in comparison to the Macintosh.

The Video Toaster

I was recently told a story about a producer who owned a one-million-dollar-plus video production studio. Not only did his company produce videos and animation for films and television, but he also rented out time in his studio to other producers. He and a few members of his company were attending a multimedia conference when they saw a demonstration of the Amiga computer with the NewTek Video Toaster installed. Graphics were flying around the screen and forming new shapes in the same impressive manner that he

An image from Todd Rundgren's "Change Myself" music video, produced at home by Rundgren using the Video Toaster.

could produce in his own million-dollar studio. When he asked about the cost of the systems involved to produce the work, he was astounded to learn that the entire setup was less than $40,000— $10,000 of which was for two Amigas with Video Toasters installed. He, on the other hand, had an investment of over one million dollars in equipment with three years remaining on the lease. After the conference, the gentleman called his people together and forbade them to ever mention the Amiga machine again. He had too much invested in more expensive technology.

Another story tells of a young animator who won a job to complete some animation for a Hollywood film. The budget for the job was $300,000—a normal charge for this type of work. The animator purchased equipment that included Amiga computers and Video Toasters and completed the job, all for a cost of about $60,000. He not only made a huge profit, but he also paid off his equipment. Working out of his home, with lower overhead, he could compete with even the largest studios. The low-cost Video Toaster, introduced in 1990, has become a hardware trigger for a new computer industry, Desktop Video (DTV).

DTV closely parallels the growth of Desktop Publishing, discussed in the beginning of this chapter. The computer transfers immense video production power into the hands of the individual computer owners, making them competitive with large companies. This transfer of power is inevitable with any new computer industry,

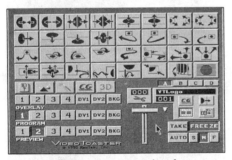

The Video Toaster's on-screen interface allows for simple operation: Just point and click with the mouse.

and the gentleman with the million dollar studio in our first story would do well to pay attention to the new developments rather than bury his head in the sand. Otherwise, his fate could be the same as that of many typesetting companies who ignored the emerging desktop publishing industry: They no longer exist.

With the Video Toaster, you can produce semi-professional video in the comfort of your own home. The NewTek Video Toaster is a low-cost video switcher with 128 special effects. Using the Amiga as a platform, you can produce your own television programs with spinning three-dimensional figures, and a host of others animations, while mixing four sources of video. The significance of the Toaster is not what it does, but its low price. Equipment with similar capabilities previously has been priced at $50,000 to $100,000. A Video Toaster board for the Amiga, including software, was introduced at about $1,500. Early in 1992, stand-alone Video Toasters that will operate with both the PC and the Mac are due on the market. Each box combines Amiga technology with the Video Toaster. It's actually another computer in a new box.

Some people have predicted that Desktop Video (DTV) will be one of the next big computer industries, similar to desktop publishing. Although it seems to be an emerging fascination, DTV is vastly more complicated than desktop publishing. There are more standards to consider, and every turn requires another piece of video or audio equipment. The possibilities are exciting.

Businesses, schools, hospitals and other organizations could produce their own videos for training and marketing purposes without the expense of major video production companies. Individual animator/producers could offer inexpensive services to those companies who have a low budget, but prefer to let someone else do the work. Anyone who owns a video camera could become an amateur video producer, greatly enhancing their own home videos.

Other Trends in Multimedia

Desktop video production is one trend in multimedia that will grow in the next 10 years, and there are numerous other possibilities.

Language Lessons: The multimedia environment is already being used to provide foreign language lessons. The *HyperGlot* Software Company produces foreign language courses on CD-ROM for the Macintosh. The courses are built around both reading and hearing the language. You can have the computer either pronounce or translate a word by merely pointing at the word and clicking the mouse button.

Interactive Magazines: In the section on laser disk technology, it's noted that *Verbum* magazine in San Diego is already publishing a magazine on CD-ROM that displays video clips, talks to the reader, plays music, and offers "artificial live-panel discussions."

Reading to Children: I've seen demonstrations of a Macintosh with a CD-ROM that reads stories to children, highlighting the words while reading. It even translates a selected word to Spanish.

Multimedia Encyclopedias: Reference and entertainment applications of all kinds will incorporate multimedia. The encyclopedias will talk. The dictionaries will tell you how to pronounce words. We will learn from animation and video sequences.

These are just a few examples of multimedia applications. In your occupation there may be many more opportunities. Most of the examples are on the Amiga and Macintosh computers because that's where the majority of the work to date has been done. But the IBM-compatible world is trying to catch up.

Microsoft and some of the other giants of the PC world have developed a multimedia standard to run under Microsoft *Windows* 3.0, including a fast PC, enhanced sound cap-

Compton's Multimedia Encyclopedia utilizes full text, pictures, sound, animation, and an on-line dictionary.

abilities, VGA high-resolution color graphics and a CD-ROM drive. Even with this standard, few expect that the movement forward will be fast. The single-processor design of even the fastest IBM-compatible computer is just too much of a bottleneck for many advanced multimedia applications. But the PC's new XGA video standard will have a separate processor for graphics. Many coprocessors are available to plug into the PC, and one high-end audio product has 12 digital signal processors that will plug into a PC slot. The strength of the PC is its expandability. Don't count it out of the multimedia race.

Multimedia applications are certainly some of the most glamorous opportunities of the next decade. They will have all the razzle-dazzle. At your first opportunity, I urge you to see a demonstration of what people are doing with multimedia computer systems. It is a stimulating experience. But don't take your checkbook with you; you may just find yourself embarked on a new career.

In spite of all the flash, multimedia systems are only a small piece of what will be occurring with computers. The more boring modem and mysterious local area network will greatly contribute to our opportunities, while PenPad-type computers will change the way we work and play.

The next section gives a glimpse into some of the technology that, though not ready to be triggers in this decade, will have significant impact in the next century.

Technology of the Next Century

Some of the technology being developed today won't have a major impact as hardware triggers until the next century. That's not to say that these technologies aren't being used today, or that there won't be significant events occurring in the next decade because of them. The delayed hardware trigger effect is because either the price of the technology is too high right now for the mass market, or not enough of the installation of the new technology will be completed by the year 2000.

Even though these advances aren't readily available to today's average computer user, knowledge of these new developments is useful in planning the new ventures of the '90s. Eventually, systems will be converting to the new technology, and those who are aware of these developments will plan to make the conversion as painless as possible.

Fiber Optics

Fiber optics will revolutionize computing and society in the next century just as the highway systems built in the '50s and '60s revolutionized travel and commerce. As fiber optics slowly replaces the older copper wiring systems, a worldwide network for information travel will spur numerous new opportunities. But it is a time-consuming, expensive process to run millions of miles of cable, and the job won't be near completion until the end of this century.

The major advantage of fiber optic cabling is the volume of data that can be transferred over the lines. Fiber optics could potentially solve many of the communications problems associated with slow data transfer. Video telephones are likely to become a reality. Video conferencing will be available to even the smallest businesses. Multimedia applications will become the standard for computer uses. The groundwork for the next generation of telecommunications is being built today.

Fiber optics is the medium of choice for long-distance data transmission. In the late '80s, the major metropolitan areas were connected with fiber optics. Major long-distance companies rely upon fiber optics for much of their service, and are continuing to lay more cable. In the early '90s the linking of Europe, North America, the Orient and other parts of the world with fiber optic cable is due to be completed.

The goals of the future for fiber optics are summed up in ISDN (Integrated Service Digital Network). All voice, high-speed data, slow-scan video and facsimile will be transmitted over the same cable. ISDN is a standard that has been agreed upon by major companies and governments to make the networking of the world easier.

The fruits of fiber optics will come into the home when houses and businesses throughout each city are networked with fiber optic cable. This worldwide network will make computers in the home as common as the telephone. Fiber optics will be the primary conduit into the home for entertainment, education, commerce and communication. Currently in the United States the telephone and cable television companies are locked in a battle for the rights to bring programming into the home. There is so much of the future at stake that the struggle is understandable.

Massive Parallel Processing

In our quest for faster and more powerful computers, there has always been a major roadblock: the processor. The primary design of most computers for the past three decades depended on one main processor to do the bulk of the work. The lone processor becomes a bottleneck when the amount of data-handling outruns the processor capabilities. On multiuser systems, this means long waits for the users if there are too many people on the system.

Most of today's computers have subordinate processors that relieve the main processor of some of its controlling functions. This helps considerably. Cray's supercomputers use up to eight high-powered processors to achieve incredible speeds of calculation. But even the Cray supercomputers are being outmatched by a different approach to computing. Smaller computer companies have taken the approach of adding thousands of microprocessors to one computer. The microprocessors work in parallel, giving speeds of operation that outrun a Cray at a much lower cost. Though many engineering and scientific companies are using computers with processor arrays, it will be at least a decade before this type of power is available to the average consumer. This is due primarily to the immense complications of programming parallel processors.

The Amiga is currently the best known low-cost multiple processor computer. This is what has given the machine its unique advantage in desktop video and multimedia applications. But multiple processor computers are the hardware of the future. Intel, the microchip giant, is currently working on a single chip that will include five processors, two coprocessors and one video coprocessor. This type of technology will be a quantum leap for desktop computing beyond the current single-processor computers of today.

But the concept of parallel computing goes well beyond the massive parallel computers of the future. In theory, a properly operated local area network uses parallel processing. The processor in the server is not the main processor in the system, but rather one of many processors that distribute the workload according to demand. Unlike the older multiuser systems where the mini or mainframe computer did all the work for each of the numerous "dumb" terminals, each computer in a network has its own processor that does most of the work; the server offers and collects data for the user while monitoring and controlling the network. With properly designed software, each computer in the network becomes a parallel processor, greatly increasing the speed and power of the entire system. This creates a synergy that gives the network a power greater than the power of the individual computers.

The organizations of the future will more likely model parallel computing than our present functional- and project-type organizations. Even though the benefits of parallel processing in computers will not be in general use until the next century, the concepts can help us design better computer networks and the better organizations we'll need in the next century.

Wide Area Networks

Distance has always been a limitation within computer systems. Much of the speed improvements of microcomputers are directly attributed to the fact that as a chip becomes smaller, the distance the information is required to travel is shorter. Networks of computers have similar limitations. Reliable transfer of data is limited by the medium of travel (copper wire or fiber optics), the amount of data that can pass over the cable, and the time it takes the data to travel the distance. The problems of Wide Area Networks are much greater than the problems of local areas networks, yet once installed, many of the limitations of geography seem to evaporate. Real-time computer communication becomes possible, providing many new opportunities for the future. Today wide area networks are being used by only the largest companies and government bodies. In the next century, the world may actually be a network of wide area networks connected to the many local area networks. The opportunities of the '90s would be greatly enhanced by this kind of worldwide communications system.

Data Compression Technology

Another approach to the problem of moving data over a great distance is to compress the data into smaller packages before it's sent. In many cases this is a great saver of transmission time, but it has its limitations. First, it consumes time to compress data. In some cases almost as much time as it does to transmit. Second, once it's received it must be decompressed before it can be used at the other end, another time-consuming process. If you want real-time information transfer, some development work remains to be done. The future of data compression shows great promise. Work is currently being done on both voice and video real-time compression and decompression.

Some people say there are limits to how much data can be compressed, though no one is sure what those limits are. If there are limits, most likely they are far beyond any boundary we can visualize today. Data compression is used today in various forms, especially to help overcome the slow speed of modems. In this decade, there could easily be major breakthroughs in data compression technology that could enhance the performance of all our communication devices. If this occurs, the fruits of desktop computer opportunities will become apparent in the next century.

There are many other areas of computer technology where work is being done to create new hardware triggers. Voice and visual recognition devices will greatly improve (and hopefully drop in price) in the next decade. Measurement devices of all kinds, for medicine, science, engineering, home security and many other applications, will come to the mass market, each triggering its own opportunities. If there are limits, no one knows where they lie. It is a matter of identifying the computer openings in your occupation and proceeding with a plan for seizing them.

The Search for More Hardware Triggers

This chapter has presented the hardware triggers that I feel are likely to generate the new computer industries of the next 10 years. There's a high probability that I've overlooked technology that will be just as important as what I've mentioned, either because I'm too shortsighted to see it, or I'm totally oblivious to it. This does not change the principles, and if you're in a position to see the new changes, seize your opportunity.

Chapter Six

The Opportunity Matrix:
An Organized Approach to Identifying
Computer Opportunities

"The hairbrained idea may well start the discussion that will lead to the perfect improvement."

—Anonymous

There is no shortage of ideas. If anything, there is an overabundance of ideas and not enough time or resources to explore them. The problem is to identify the best idea for your strengths and focus your energies in that direction. The following is an exercise designed to help you do just that: identify the ideas best for you, and focus your efforts in that direction. This exercise can be done alone or with a group of people who have similar interests and backgrounds. It can be done on paper, a chalkboard or a computer. It is a brainstorming exercise that will help you create numerous possibilities.

Initially, some of the ideas will seem outrageous. Stick with them and continue their expansion; they may soon turn into very real possibilities. During the exercise, generate your ideas without continuous evaluation. If you evaluate the ideas too soon, you may kill the creative process that will bring you even more opportunities. If you do evaluate during the session, do so in a positive manner. Don't state, "It'll never work!" but rather use questions like, "How can we make that idea work?" or "How can we add more to this concept?" Avoid the thought, "I don't think that will work because . . . " The future is built with what *can* be done, not with what can't.

In the exercise you will be cross-indexing the concepts of computer productivity with the available hardware triggers as they apply to your area of concern. The first step is to create a matrix on paper, chalkboard or computer. Across the horizontal axis list the productivity concepts.

Computer Productivity

The basic concepts of computer productivity discussed in Chapter Four are listed here for your quick reference:

Collaboration—Rather than working alone on a problem, we interact with others, exchanging ideas and questions, thereby building on the work of others.

Physical Mobility—In our travels, we carry our tools of information with us, accessing data at great geographic distances.

Information Mobility—Rather than traveling with the computer, the information comes to the user. Any way, anytime are the key words.

Interactive—The computer system reacts, probes and stimulates the user. Rather than being a passive receptor of information and programming, the computer becomes the active partner in an endeavor.

Specialization—Bodies of knowledge in very specialized areas and applications are produced by a very narrow use of the computer.

Mass Customization—Products and services are tailored to the individual while offering the economies of scale of mass production.

Generalized Details—Volumes of details are recast into a bigger picture, allowing patterns and trends to be readily identified.

Stimulation—Computer technology is applied to the techniques for stimulating human creativity—new views of old problems.

Visualization—Painting scenarios of possibilities.

Strategy—Extrapolating the big picture into possible alternative directions and plans.

Human Limitations—Problems of human limitations are opportunities for the future. Who will invent the first five-fingered computer?

Save Time—One of the standards of computer productivity.

Increase Results—One of the standards of computer productivity.

These concepts serve as stimulators for the possibilities of the future. List these across the horizontal axis of your matrix as shown in Figure 1.

Hardware Triggers
The next step is to list the hardware triggers on the vertical axis. Chapter Five explains the possible hardware triggers in more detail. The following is an abbreviated list of hardware triggers for quick reference:

Modem—The modem is a device that, when attached to a computer, allows the computer to communicate with one or more other computers via the telephone lines.

Local Area Network—A LAN is a system of computers, connected via cable in a relatively small area, in which the computers interact or communicate either with each other or via a server computer.

Voice Mail—Voice Mail is a expansion capability that, when added to a PC, allows the answering, routing and recording of incoming calls while offering voice information to the caller.

Laser Disk Drive—Laser Disk Drives belong to the family of removable optical mass storage technology that allows the huge volumes of data needed for expert systems, graphics, voice and audio, and other applications to be stored on the same diskette.

PenPad-Type Computer—PenPad-type computers are the new family of computers that allow the mobile or graphic-oriented user to work in a manner much more suitable to the ergonomics of the human, i.e. the pen and paper.

Opportunity Matrix

	Collaboration	Physical Mobility	Information Mobility	Interactive

Figure 1. List the basic concepts of computer productivity across the horizontal axis of your matrix.

High Resolution Color Monitors—Computer monitors that are starting to approach the resolution of the human eye.

Color Printers—Computer printing equipment capable of reproducing on paper the color images on the computer screen.

Scanners (Grayscale and Color)—Equipment capable of capturing art or a photograph and converting it into a computer-usable format for later modification or use.

Sounds Cards—Audio capabilities in a computer that make possible the reproduction of voice, sound effects and music.

Voice Control—Hardware that allows the control of computers by input from the human voice.

Video Toaster—Computer-controlled hardware device that, when used in conjunction with other video and audio devices, allows the production of professional-looking videos without an expensive production studio.

Fax—Equipment, either stand-alone or an expansion to a PC, that will transmit paper images from one location to another fax machine via the telephone lines.

List the hardware triggers across the horizontal axis as shown in Figure 2.

Focusing on Strengths

It is now important to narrow your focus to your strengths. If you are an artist or have a knack for writing short verse, you may decide to explore the opportunities in greeting cards. Your focus should be your area of expertise and experience (i.e. crime, education, medicine, etc.). If you select an area as broad as education, try to narrow it down further to a category like foreign languages or reading. Regardless of how narrowly you define your area of emphasis, you will be surprised at the number of ideas generated.

In the corner of your chart write your focus area. (If you are

Opportunity Matrix

	Collaboration	Physical Mobility	Information Mobility	Interactive
Modem				
Local Area Network				
Voice Mail				
Laser Disk Drive				
PenPad-Type Computer				
Color Printer				

Figure 2. List hardware triggers down the vertical axis of your matrix.

planning to brainstorm more than one focus area, create a separate chart for each area, as each new direction will yield different results.)

You have now created the matrix. Each productivity concept should be separated by a vertical line extending to the bottom of the chart. Each hardware trigger should be separated by a horizontal line that extends to the end of the chart. This has created a matrix of boxes for cross indexing and generating ideas.

Note: If you have other productivity concepts or potential hardware triggers not discussed in this book, by all means add them. This system works equally well for any new entries. Only the results will vary, which, after all, is your goal.

We will use the greeting card business as an example. While working your matrix, you should mentally substitute your focus area anytime greeting cards are mentioned.

Start with the first concept, "Collaboration," on the horizontal axis. (There is nothing sacred about the order of the concepts on the horizontal axis or the hardware triggers on the vertical. Start at the point you prefer.) Scan down each hardware trigger and ask yourself, "How can this type of computer hardware impact my focus area?" As the ideas pop into your head, quickly jot down notes in the associated box (see Figure 3). If the box is too small, put down abbreviations and add more extensive notes to a separate piece of paper headed with the name of the productivity concept and the hardware trigger (Figure 4). If nothing pops into your head at any given box, forget it and move on. There are plenty more boxes to review, and in most cases you'll have more ideas than you'll ever be able to handle.

In our example, under Modems and Collaboration we brainstorm that a group of customers could help tailor a birthday card from various remote locations. In Figure 4 we've noted more of the details of the concept.

Next to Local Area Network we have written down the idea of both the greeting card "signers" and an artist being able to work on the card simultaneously.

Under Physical Mobility and next to Laser Disk Drive, we have cards being printed at remote locations, like fairs or shopping malls. The CD-ROM makes the cards easily transportable in any quantity.

Opportunity Matrix

	Collaboration	Physical Mobility	Information Mobility	Interactive
Modem	Several people help to tailor a birthday card from a remote distance		Computerized Greeting Cards sent by the phone	
Local Area Network	An artist and a writer simultaneously work on the same card			
Voice Mail				Greeting cards that talk back via the phone
Laser Disk Drive		Greeting cards are stored on CD for printing at remote locations		
PenPad-Type Computer				
Color Printer				

Figure 3. As you match hardware triggers to computer productivity concepts, jot down notes in the associated box.

Greeting Cards
Collaboration–Modems

A business is organized that offers collaborative greeting cards. Customers who will "sign" the card call in at their convenience, either via telephone, voice mail or modem, to give their input on the card. The computer then generates the tailored card, and sends it on to the recipient via mail, fax, or other available medium.

Figure 4. Add more extensive notes to a separate piece of paper if the boxes on your matrix prove too small.

Under Information Mobility and next to Modem, we have conceived a business that will send greeting cards anywhere via modem. Maybe cards could be purchased in computer format via modem.

Under Interactive and across from Voice Mail, we have generated an idea for a greeting card that interacts with the recipient. The voice card is delivered via the telephone, and the audio messages change according to the buttons the recipient pushes on the phone pad. Each message could be in the sender's own voice or voices.

Under Specialization and opposite Laser Disk Drive, the business of selling a business could be envisioned. Software on CD-ROM for producing greeting cards could be sold to young entrepreneurs pursuing one of the other greeting card ideas. There would be updates and new cards to be sold to these new businesses every season.

Under Mass Customization and lined up with Laser Disk Drive, you might list that standard-format greeting cards could be sold that are tailored for the individual and printed on a full-color printer, another hardware trigger. Maybe the individual cards would be sold at shopping malls or county fairs.

You may notice that many of the ideas overlap with others, or that you need to combine the hardware triggers into different categories. Don't hesitate to move items and thoughts as necessary to develop an idea. This is a free-form tool for thought generation.

Some matrix blocks may remain blank. That's okay. If the cross between a hardware trigger and a concept doesn't immediately trigger ideas, move on. A spark can't be forced. It's either there or it isn't.

After you've brainstormed as many blocks as possible, go back and star those items that seem particularly exciting. The ideas that ignite your enthusiasm are likely to be your best opportunities. List these ideas on another piece of paper.

Take each of your starred items and develop them into a vision of how the systems would work. Who would use the system? How would users interact with the system? What hardware would be needed to build the system? What software would be required? What other types of occupations would be spawned by this new system?

Now, list your strengths, either as an individual or as a company or group. Match those strengths to the different facets of your new system. The areas where your new strengths match up are your new computer opportunities. The areas where your strengths don't match up with the new system are opportunities for others, maybe the others you need to collaborate with on your new venture. Part of the work may be finding these collaborators.

Prepare a list of steps that must be taken to start moving in your new direction. This is the beginning of your new action plan: a living document that not only includes your goals, but also how you will achieve them.

The final point is to pick only one idea for your present future. The biggest marketing and business mistake made by most new ventures is attempting to do too many things at the same time. It will be necessary to focus your resources to achieve maximum results. Do first things first, then you will be in a position to consider the other ideas.

Chapter Seven
Regrets

"Inspirations never go in for long engagements; they demand immediate marriage to action."
—Brenden Francis

As you've discovered by now, ideas are cheap. There is no shortage of inspiration, only a shortage of people who are willing to pursue it. Ideas only come to fruition through persistent work. If you have uncovered a brilliant idea, there is a good chance that someone else is already pursuing it. Or is there? Maybe *they'll* give it up because they believe that someone else is pursuing it. Or maybe they won't do it as well as you would.

How many times have you had an idea, only to find it produced and selling on the market six months later? "I thought of that!" What's the difference between you and the people who made the idea work? Not as much as you may think. They probably didn't have any more time or money. They weren't any smarter than you. In fact, there was only one major difference between you and them: They did it and you didn't. In fact, you probably didn't even start.

That's the first rule: If you want to finish, you must start! No one in history ever finished anything without first starting. Most people seem to be waiting for something to come to them, and then they're surprised when nothing does. Maybe your start is buying your first computer, or that new software package for your old computer. It isn't luck; get started!

The second rule is do something that moves you in the direction of your idea every day. It doesn't have to be a big step, but something should be done. Maybe you just sit in front of your computer for 15 minutes. At least if you're sitting there the odds of you actually accomplishing something are greater than if you're asleep in front of the television. It's amazing how often you will actually start working.

The final rule is stay focused. Envision your dream as often as possible during the day. Let it become an obsession. The more the goal becomes a part of you, the closer it gets to becoming a reality.

This has been a book of fiction and fantasies, but the future always starts with dreams. These are not impossible dreams, but dreams based in the very real technology of today: achievable dreams. The number one regret people have as they enter their later years is that they didn't take more risks and pursue their dreams. They regret what they didn't do. To be sure, there are no guarantees that any new idea will be successful, but what do you want to regret: the things you did, or the things you didn't do?

Appendix A

Future Computer Opportunities
Resources

The following is a list of some of the companies and products that were researched during the writing of this book. It is by no means a complete list of all the multimedia hardware and software, pen-based computing technology, and other cutting-edge computer technology available; rather, it is a mere sampling of what the computer industry is capable of producing now and in the next 10 years.

Miscellaneous

ducorp Computer Services
7434 Trade Street, San Diego, CA 92121
(619) 536-9999

Product: An international computer product mail-order company offering more than 10,000 public domain and shareware programs for Macintosh computers. CD-ROM titles and drives, computer accessories and commercial software for Mac, IBM PC and compatible computers are also offered.

GVC Technologies, Inc.
99 Demarest Road, Sparta, NJ 07871
(201) 579-3630

Product: The FMM-9624 pocket fax/modem, a portable device that combines a 9600 bps group III send/receive fax with a 2400 bps V.42bis/MNP data modem; will extend the communications reach of laptop, portable and notebook computer users.

Image-In Incorporated
406 East 79th Street, Minneapolis, MN 55420
(612) 888-3633

Product: *Image-In-Color*—A *Windows*-based 24-bit color photo-retouching system which enables users to enhance, rotate, crop, stretch and edit photographs from the Kodak Photo CD.

Multimedia

Hardware

Cardinal Technologies, Inc.
1827 Freedom Road, Lancaster, PA 17601
(717) 293-3000

Product: SOUNDVision—A complete multimedia PC upgrade adapter, combining super VGA, stereo sound and all the interfaces required for CD-ROM and multimedia peripherals.

Commodore Business Machines, Inc.
1200 Wilson Drive, West Chester, PA 19380
(215) 431-9100

Product: The Amiga Computer for multimedia computing.

Creative Labs, Inc.
2050 Duane Avenue, Santa Clara, CA 95054
(408) 986-1461

Product: Sound Blaster, Sound Blaster Pro, Multimedia Upgrade Kit—Sound Blaster is the "ultimate" sound board that is an all-in-one speech, music, voice, MIDI and game port. Sound Blaster Pro is the multimedia sound standard that includes stereo, music, voice, speech, MIDI, CD-ROM interface, and game port. The Multimedia Upgrade Kit is an all-in-one multimedia solution, including Sound Blaster Pro, a MIDI kit, CD-ROM Drive and multimedia software.

Genesis Integrated Systems, Inc.
1000 Shelard Parkway, Suite 270, Minneapolis, MN 55426-4918
(612) 544-4445

Product: GenSTAR 3000 Series CD-ROM Drives.

International Business Machines
Corporation (IBM)
IBM United States, Department 7 EY
4111 Northside Parkway, Atlanta, GA 30327

Product: Multimedia PC system, "Ultimedia" multimedia solutions.

JVC Information Products Company
of America
19900 Beach Blvd., Suite 1, Huntington Beach, CA 92648
(714) 965-2610

Product: The industry's first "write-once" internal CD-ROM drive; in the future the drive will support multiple session recording.

Microsoft Corporation
One Microsoft Way, Redmond, WA 98052-6399
(206) 882-8080

Product: Multimedia PC systems.

NEC Technologies Inc.
1255 Michael Drive, Wood Dale, IL 60191
(708) 860-9500

Product: Intersect CD-ROM Reader; Portable CD-ROM Reader
(see also "PenPad-Type Computing").

NewTek Incorporated
215 S.E. Eighth St., Topeka, KS 66603
(913) 354-1146

Product: The Video Toaster desktop video production system.

Philips Consumer Electronics
One Philips Drive
P.O. Box 14810, Knoxville, TN 37914-1810
(615) 521-4316

Product: Compact Disc–Interactive Information Systems.

Software

Britannica Software
310 South Michigan Avenue, Chicago, IL 60604
(312) 347-7135

Product: *Compton's Multimedia Encyclopedia*—A multimedia encyclopedia for utilizing full text, pictures, sound, animation, and an
on-line dictionary (for IBM-compatible PCs under *Windows* 3.0).

First Byte
3100 S. Harbor Blvd., Suite 150, Santa Ana, CA 92704
(714) 432-1740

Product: *Monologue* for *Windows*: Provides speech capability to
any PC; converts text strings to speech signals, and then plays the
signals through an internal or auxiliary speaker.

The Hyperglot Software Company
505 Forest Hills Blvd., Knoxville, Tennessee 37919

Product: *Learn to Speak Spanish*—A complete Spanish course
on CD-ROM.

Innotech
#107 Silver Star Blvd., Scarborough, Ontario, Canada M1V 5A2
(416) 321-3838

Product: *FindIt* and *BuildIt*—Fast, powerful CD-ROM retrieval engines that have been used with nearly 150 different CD-ROM databases. (For UNIX, PC and Macintosh.)

Interactive Image Technologies Ltd.
908 Niagra Falls Boulevard, North Tonawanda, NY 14120-2060
(416) 361-0333

Product: *Hypercase*, The Hypermedia Construction Kit—a tool that lets you build interactive programs, creating even complex programs via the built-in language HyperLang.

Jasmine Multimedia Publishing Company
1888 Century Park East, Suite 300, Los Angeles, CA 90067
(213) 277-7523

Product: Jasmine Stock Video Library—The first collection of video and production music available to software and multimedia producers, featuring thousands of hours of high-quality video and hundreds of professionally scored and recorded audio selections on compact discs.

MapInfo Corporation
200 Broadway, Troy, NY 12180
(518) 274-8673

Product: *MapInfo*—Offers desktop mapping software that integrates database information with maps for dynamic, powerful data visualization and analysis. Maps can be edited and printed to present applications such as sales territory analysis, demographic analysis, transportation dispatch, site locations and more. (For *Windows*, Macintosh, DOS, Sun and HP.)

Metatec Corporation
7001 Discovery Blvd., Dublin, OH 43017
(614) 761-2000

Product: *Nautilus*, a multimedia, CD-ROM-based magazine that enables subscribers to access and contribute information, software, games, music and commentary.

Midisoft Corporation
P.O. Box 1000, Bellevue, WA 98009
(206) 881-7176

Product: *Midisoft Studio* for *Windows*: a complete, professional

MIDI recording studio that allows you to see and edit notes on a
music staff as you play.

Passport Designs Inc.
625 Miramontes St., Half Moon Bay, CA 94019
(415) 726-0280

Product: Trax 2.0/Master Tracks Pro—Trax is a desktop MIDI
recording studio. Master Tracks Pro is a professional MIDI
sequencing program providing a powerful tool for recording and
playing back songs, sound tracks and musical compositions. (For
IBM PCs with *Windows* and Macintosh Computers.)

Optical Disk Drives

Maxoptix Corporation
2520 Junction Avenue, San Jose, CA 95134
(408) 954-9711

Product: The Tahiti family of Erasable Optical Disk Drives.

Plasmon Data Systems, Inc.
1654 Centre Point Drive, Milpitas, CA 95035
(408) 956-9400

Product: A multifunction Optical Disk Drive, instantly compatible
with most operating systems.

PenPad-Type Computing

Go Corporation
950 Tower Lane, 14th Floor, Foster City, CA 94404
(415) 345-7400

Product: Penpoint Operating System.

Grid Systems
P.O. Box 5003, Fremont, CA 94537-5003
(415) 656-4700

Product: GRiDPad, the industry's first pen-based computer.
Supports both PenPoint and *Windows* for Pen Computing, as well
as an MS-DOS-based GRiDPen operating environment.

MicroTouch Systems, Inc.
55 Jonspin Road, Wilmington, MA 01887
(508) 694-9900

Product: TouchPen—The first pen-computing digitizer that
supports both finger and stylus input.

Momenta Corporation
295 North Bernardo Avenue, Mountain View, CA 94043
(415) 969-3876

Product: "Pentop" computer, using an electronic stylus that writes
directly on a flat-panel screen. This computer can also serve as a
traditional laptop or notebook-style computer using an attachable
keyboard and running standard MS-DOS or *Windows* software.

NCR Corporation
United States Group, P.O. Box 606, Dayton, OH 45401-8967
1-800-225-5627

Product: The NCR 3125 NotePad Computer. (Can utilize the
PenPoint Operating System and Microsoft *Windows* for Pen
Computing.)

NEC Technologies Inc.
1414 Massachusetts Avenue, Boxborough, MA 01719
(508) 264-8000

Product: The UltraLite SL/20 Series of notebook computers,
capable of supporting pen input. (See also "Multimedia Hardware.")

Research Data Analysis, Inc.
450 Enterprise Court, Bloomfield Hills, MI 48302
(313) 332-5000

Product: GRiDPad software

Wacom Technology Corporation
444 Castro Street, Suite 400, Mountain View, CA 94041
(415) 960-1800

Product: Pen-based computer systems with cordless, battery-free
pen technology.

Virtual Reality

StrayLight Corporation
150 Mount Bethel Road, Warren, NJ 07059
(908) 580-0086

Product: StrayLight Photo VR System.

The Vivid Group
317 Adelaide Street West, Toronto, Ontario, Canada M5V 1P9
(418) 340-9290

Product: Mandala Virtual Reality System.

Index

T

technology
    and crime prevention, 42
    and education, 40
    and entertainment, 37
    and environmental issues, 43
    and hardware triggers, 23
    and health and medicine, 47
    and media, 19, 44
    and the future, 109
The Vivid Group, 132
TouchPen, 96, 131
Trax, 131

U

UNIX, 24

V

Verbum Magazine, 91
video toaster, 30, 31, 53, 105, 106, 119
virtual reality, 103
visualization, 67, 116
voice control, 100, 119
voice mail, 28, 31, 83, 85
voice recognition, 31

W

Wacom Technology Corporation, 132
Wide Area Networks, 112
Windows, 24
    for Pen Computing, 94
working relationships, 17
workstations, 24

Other Books From
Computer Publishing Enterprises:

PC Secrets
Tips and Tricks to Increase Your Computer's Power
by R. Andrew Rathbone

Future Computer Opportunities
Visions of Computers Into the Year 2000
by Jack Dunning

Software Buying Secrets
by Wally Wang

DOS Secrets
by Dan Gookin

101 Computer Business Ideas
by Wally Wang

Digital Dave's Computer Tips and Secrets
A Beginner's Guide to Problem Solving
by Roy Davis

The Best FREE Time-Saving Utilities for the PC
by Wally Wang

How to Get Started With Modems
by Jim Kimble

How to Make Money With Computers
by Jack Dunning

Rookie Programming
A Newcomer's Guide to Programming in BASIC, C, and Pascal
by Ron Dippold

Hundreds of Fascinating and Unique Ways to Use Your Computer
by Tina Rathbone

The Computer Gamer's Bible
by R. Andrew Rathbone

Beginner's Guide to DOS
by Dan Gookin

Computer Entrepreneurs
People Who Built Successful Businesses Around Computers
by Linda Murphy

How to Understand and Buy Computers
By Dan Gookin

Parent's Guide to Educational Software and Computers
by Lynn Stewart and Toni Michael

The Official Computer Widow's (and Widower's) Handbook
by Experts on Computer Widow/Widowerhood

For more information about these books, call 1-800-544-5541.